10 Smart Moves

for Women
Who Want to Succeed
in Love and Life

By
Dianna Booher

Ten Smart Moves for Women Who Want to Succeed in Love and Life
ISBN 1-57757-016-2
Copyright © 1997 by Dianna Booher
4001 Gateway Drive
Colleyville, TX 76034-5917

Published by Trade Life Books, Inc.
P. O. Box 55325
Tulsa, Oklahoma 74155

Published in association with the literary agency of Alive Communications, Inc.,
1465 Kelly Johnson Boulevard, Suite 320, Colorado Springs, CO 80920.

Table of Contents
10 Smart Moves for Women

Acknowledgements

I'd like to express my sincerest appreciation to the following successful, smart women who granted interviews for this book, along with others who shared their experiences and insights but wish to remain anonymous. Their credentials, achievements, and successes would be too numerous to list here, but they are mentioned throughout the book, along with their comments. These women have shared deep insights and intimate glimpses of themselves. The success of the book belongs to them.

Laurie Barringer

Jo Ann Blackmon

Jeannine Brannon

Betty Bradley

Judith Briles, Ph.D.

Jane Brimmer

Terry Broomfield

Chris Casady

Angie Casey

Martha Castillo

Carolyn Corbin, Ph.D.

Katy Crane

Dru Scott, Ph.D.

Kathy Darling

Barbara Durand

Candace Elkins

Eloise Fields, Ph.D.

Lynelle Goff Eddins

Pat Greek

Dora Grider

Morgan Hall

Jane Handly, CSP and CPAE

Kathy Harless

Debbie Henderson

Debbie Hertzog

Hattie Hill

Sallie Hightower, Ph.D.

Gail Jones, Ph.D.

Gay Knight

Nancy Koenig

Susan Lanigan

Cynthia Latham

Sue Morris

Sheri Nasca

Amy Newman

Rebecca Noecker

Jeanne O'Connor-Green

Lisa Porterfield

Myra Puryear

Jennifer Raymond

Lynne Ritchie

Amy Rudy

Ann-Marie Stephens

Iris Torvik, Ph.D.

Deborah Tyler

Vicky Weinberg

Trudy White

Teresa Withrow

Michele Wong-Ota

Kathleen Wu

Stephanie Zweben

Introduction

Not too long ago a law firm phoned to invite me to speak to a retreat of female attorneys and their clients. During a conference call with several of the attorneys planning the event, we began to discuss various motivational topics. One attorney made this comment: "Whatever you say, just be upbeat. We don't want you to talk about what we need to do to 'fix' ourselves as women. We're tired of hearing all that. Let's focus on the positives for the weekend."

I agree. There has been much too much emphasis on what's broken and not enough on what's right with our lives. So what are those positives? Those smart moves for women?

Because the majority of women have moved out of the role of traditional stay-at-home wife, they have different pressures, different issues, different decisions, and different lifestyles from the lives they saw modeled by their own mothers. Consider the sheer number of women now in the work force: 62 percent. Currently, there are 7.7 million women-owned businesses generating in excess of $1.4 trillion annually and employing more people than the Fortune 500 companies.

Fifty-one percent of all mothers with children at home hold full-time jobs, and another 18 percent of mothers work outside the home part-time. More than half of all professional and managerial positions are now held by women, and it seems as if the trend of the last four decades will continue — more than half of all college degrees now go to women.

Beyond the world of female business owners, those women working for others are experiencing employment jitters and longer hours. Women are seeking some sort of relief — if not physical relief from the long hours and hectic pace, then mental release and spiritual perspective.

I'm writing for all women, those of us who are just graduating from college and those who are aging babyboomers, those who have experienced a family breakup and those who have been married fifty years to the same man, those who feel the empty-nest syndrome after all of life has been devoted to children and those who are childless, those who have had no career and now want one and those who pursued a career and missed a family. Common to all of us — whether twenty-six or seventy-six — is the questioning about spiritual mission, meaningful work, and intimate relationships.

Women engage in a lifelong search for fulfillment through intimacy, and that search often begins outside themselves. They expect the men in their lives to make them complete and keep them happy. That failing, they bury themselves in their children's lives or in their jobs. When their men, their children, or their jobs reject, ignore, or bore them, women feel empty, used up, disappointed, or depressed.

That's the "why" behind this book — a search for those smart moves to make women feel content, useful, and accomplished. I talked in-depth to women from all walks of life, of all academic backgrounds, of all ages, and of several cultures. Their spiritual perspectives ranged from no belief in God, to seeking God, to born-again Christians. They have offered some advice and insights about their wins and losses through the years and shared their views on career and personal success. (Note the survey summary in the Appendix.)

What do I mean by success? That definition varies from individual to individual. In fact, that's one of the smart moves discussed in Chapter 3 — defining success in your own terms. For some women, success means fulfillment through personal development. For others, success means fulfillment through career advancement and options. For others, success means fulfillment through enjoying their family and friends. For still others, success means giving their lives in service to others and God.

Success for too many of us means having it all. Consequently, we never let ourselves *feel* successful, because who, in this life, can feel as though they have accomplished all — or even enough? Certainly none of the smart women I spoke with felt they have reached their fullest potential. They all talked about being on a journey of continual learning, of growing insights, and of their desire and struggle to make a difference in the world.

This book is about that trip — understanding the hopes and fears, the triumphs and tragedies, and the successes and failures of other women. In doing so, we gain understanding about ourselves. As many philosophers and writers have already observed, we will never live long enough to make all the mistakes and master all the opportunities ourselves. Instead, smart women learn from other people's experiences. The smart women interviewed for this book have been candid and cordial in telling about their pain and gain, and their tears and joys along the way.

After I listened to their stories about their feelings, dreams, frustrations, regrets, and joys, I compiled this list of smart principles for relationships and careers that lead to personal satisfaction and success:

Master your moods. This first chapter acknowledges that women experience a wide range of moods. It suggests that life goes better when we control these moods to motivate ourselves and others, rather than let the moods undermine our decisions, our actions, and our advancement. The discussion helps pinpoint the symptoms and the causes for that "overwhelmed" feeling.

Seek a sense of self-worth. Chapter 2 focuses on how important our self-concept is to our work and our relationships. Low self-esteem affects most women at some point in their lives — during their dating years, after a job loss or business failure, during an abusive relationship, in the midst of a struggle with poor health, or in a tug-of-war with a wayward teen. Having a sense of self comes from constructing several pillars in our lives, not just one platform. Multiple pillars provide added security when destructive winds blow.

Set sail on your own seas. Many women have been sailing along in pursuit of someone else's goals — their spouse's, their child's, or a parent's. Then they wonder why their life is less than fulfilling. This chapter is about getting in touch with what you yourself feel passionate about so that you can feel genuine satisfaction as you sail through life.

Put up or shut up. We have a chance to say yes or no each time we approach a fork in the road. Some of us stand at that fork much too long, paralyzed by indecision and fear. This chapter is about evaluating risks and finding the courage to take a difficult, risky step. Once we've made the leap of faith, we need the discipline and emotional strength to perform, without excuse. It's scary, but smart.

Follow through on feedback. Smart women don't pout, balk, or crumble under criticism. In fact, they seek feedback to clarify their goals, correct their course, and continue to grow as human beings. This chapter offers encouragement by relating incidents in which others have learned from sometimes scathing criticism to become even more successful and satisfied in their careers and relationships.

Entertain only ethical choices. Ask 99 out of 100 people whether they typically do the "right" thing or make the morally correct choice, and I am convinced you will get a "yes" answer. But the phrase to ponder is "typically." It's those tough decisions where there's no policy or precedent that snare us, and most such decisions are like quicksand. This chapter outlines some quagmires to be wary of along the way.

Relish relationships. How many times in the last six months have you had lunch or dinner with friends? When is the last time you visited more than an hour with someone not in your immediate family? Would you take the time to attend someone's funeral that you haven't talked with in the last year? Why? Most of us want to hold on to relationships in times of tragedy; we just can't find the time to enjoy these relationships in our day-to-day lives. Worse, some of us have unresolved conflict with a child, a sister, a parent, or a spouse that's like a low-grade fever in our lives. It keeps us from feeling mentally free to enjoy the rest of our lives without guilt and regret. This chapter reflects on the value of relationships to our mental and emotional health.

Bend so you don't break. We know that bad things happen to good people. The key to understanding and surviving the frustrations and tragedies in our lives is a flexible attitude. This chapter will inspire you with courageous acts and uplifting attitudes from those women who have found themselves facing crises in health, marriage, career, or finances.

Seek spiritual certainties. From the meaningless mass suicides of cult members to the compassionate, selfless service of Mother Teresa, the spiritual side of life has perplexed many people. This chapter highlights the attention smart women have paid to their spiritual development and what the spiritual dimension adds to their lives.

Swim in the seasons of life. Some people have been swimming upstream all their lives. In whatever situations they have found themselves, it seems that everybody else is doing something different, has something different, or wants something different. Impatience and a sour outlook can become a way of life. This chapter serves as a reminder that timing means everything in enjoying life, and feeling gratitude despite the circumstances we are experiencing in the present.

As you make your way through life, I welcome your own additions to the list of smart moves. Smart women share their successes and insights.

A Note From Me to You

Let me get more personal.

- Do you ever feel as though you have lost your center, that things are swirling around you so fast you can't keep up?
- Do you ever feel "used up" emotionally?
- Do you have dreams you've never acted on?
- Do you ever doubt that you "have what it takes"?
- Do you frequently agonize over tough decisions?
- Do you feel hurt or sad when people misunderstand your actions or misjudge your intentions?
- Do you wish you had more close friendships or wish you had more time to spend with the friends you have?
- Do you regret ill feelings and strained relationships with members of your family?
- Have you ever felt discouraged in having to endure unfair situations or tragedies?
- Have you ever wondered, "Am I normal?"
- Would you like to be more successful?
- Have you ever felt that you wanted to make a stronger mark on the world and contribute more to the lives of others?

If you've answered "yes" to some or most of these questions (as I have), then I've plunged into this book for both of us.

A few months ago, after an interview on *Good Morning America* for my earlier book, *Get a Life Without Sacrificing Your Career,* I left the studio in a cloud of euphoria. The limo driver delivered me back to my hotel to retrieve my bags for the trip home. Several people stopped me as I crossed the lobby with, "Weren't you just on TV?" I nodded and smiled.

But by the time I got back on the airplane headed to Dallas, my three minutes of fame, once again, had come and gone. As I walked into my office later that afternoon, there was a brief round of "Hi, how's it going?" and then back to work. There were a mere three congratulatory faxes on my desk. Then the first person stepped into my office, "Did you know they didn't flash the book title on the screen? They only *said* it. Without seeing the title, probably nobody's going to remember it until they get to the bookstore. Next time, you ought to make sure they are going to hold the cover on the screen longer because...."

And from there, the comments went downhill. In a matter of minutes, I called an author friend in tears. After three months of criss-crossing the country doing a marathon of interviews, from small radio stations in Anchorage, Alaska, to Atlanta's CNN, to New York's *Cosmopolitan,* to the Naples, Florida, roving reporter who caught me at a convention, all the weariness came pouring out. I was so overcome with tears of disappointment that a knot welled up in my throat, and for a few moments I couldn't speak. Why could I not be "successful"? Why did I blow this latest opportunity? How could I be so dumb as to let that happen? What else did I expect?

This book has been my attempt to settle issues in my own past and gain perspective about the future.

At that moment, I needed perspective.

Have you ever been in a similar spot? Have you experienced the thrill of achieving a goal, and then within minutes felt like you were at the bottom of the mountain, staring up at yet another weary climb — one that you weren't sure you could complete?

This book has been my attempt to settle issues in my own past and gain perspective about the future. I hope the insights shared here from these smart women will settle similar issues and even raise serious questions for you.

I have a hunch that you and I — no matter our age, occupation, or family situation — are not all that unfamiliar with each other's days, dreams, and disappointments. Take risk-taking, for example. I hate to take risks and make difficult decisions. I take them. But I despise them.

I remember landing my first consulting contract back in 1980. Shell Oil contracted me to train their engineers to write technical reports. I was scheduled for six consecutive Mondays. The risk? I had only one business suit. So I waited until after the first Monday to see how they liked what I had to say before I bought another suit for the second Monday. Then I waited until after the second Monday to buy the third suit. After the third Monday, I decided to rotate the same three suits again just in case the current success was a fluke and I never won another contract.

Even today risk-taking is still not much easier for me.

You may also identify with my first financial crisis — becoming the sole support of two teens who liked to eat, wanted Christmas presents like those their friends received, and needed a college education.

But the most thought-provoking situation that we probably share is death. A few years ago my Uncle Jack died. When my dad called to give me the news, he asked if I would like to ride to the funeral with him and Mother. No, the death didn't seem like a great loss to me; in fact, that was the problem. You see, Uncle Jack was my granddad's brother, a favorite uncle that I remembered primarily from my childhood. He had a farm with a fishing tank, and two or three times a year when I was "vacationing" with my grandparents, we would go to Uncle Jack's to fish and play house with my cousin Barbara.

I considered the funeral invitation, but so many years had passed since I was a child of eight or ten. I hadn't seen him in twenty years, although I had admired him from a distance. My aunt Exa developed Alzheimer's in her early forties. So Uncle Jack devoted his last thirty years to caring for her. He hired a lady to stay with her while he farmed during the day. Then at night he took over, feeding, bathing, and exercising her until her death thirty-something years later. Through the family stories of his devotion to her during those years, I grew to admire him from afar.

But I didn't know him really. That was the sense of regret I felt the day my dad called with the news about Uncle Jack. Why go to the funeral of someone you didn't have time to interact with while they were living?

That was the beginning of some serious reflection on my part about the pace of life and the place of relationships, especially those of friends and family. And there was a deeper thought and wonder: What kind of love could a man have for a woman who he would spend thirty years caring for her every need without her even recognizing who he was?

The suits. The finances. The funeral. With this book, I am betting you have experienced some of these same feelings at various forks in the road. In my research and reflection, I wanted to explore genuine success, real satisfaction, and meaningful, motivating intimacy.

What do I want for you as readers? That you will:

- Gain the impetus to take the risk and make a decision that will open new doors of opportunity for you.

- Take initiative in seeking feedback that will strengthen your character and your performance.

- Gain courage in enduring unfair or difficult circumstances.

- Gain strength in the face of heartbreaking tragedy.

- Mend strained relationships and reclaim family and friends.

- Get in touch with the spiritual dimensions of your life to build an inner strength that will support you in times of both joy and disappointment.

- Gain insights from your failures and applaud your successes.

Please let me know if I have succeeded as you make smart moves toward personal fulfillment.

Dianna Booher

1
Master Your Moods

If there's any one charge leveled against women more often than others, it's that we're "emotional." This is a comment not only from men, but also from women about themselves. That description isn't necessarily bad!

On the contrary, because women are emotional, they often make better managers. They can identify and empathize with the feelings of their employees, build consensus for difficult decisions, gain their confidence and buy-in on tough projects, and motivate others to achieve their best. Emotions make women whole people; without emotions we would be machines. Emotionless people become criminal psychopaths. It's only when we lead our lives by emotion or let our emotions sabotage our work and relationships that trouble sets in.

Smart women master their moods; that is, they live by direction, decision, and determination rather than whim. They demonstrate self-control and commitment.

Anger, sadness, joy, fear, relief, amusement, pride, trust, kindness, jealousy, hurt, adoration, irritability, animosity, resentment, delight, love, fury — these emotions are all part of the human experience. The difficulty comes when we can't identify the feeling, don't understand its intensity, can't control its impulses, can't reduce the stress it causes, and don't know the difference between *feeling* the emotion and *acting* on the emotion.

Take anger, for example. The average person can feel

Smart women...live by direction, decision, and determination rather than whim.

anger at the grocery store clerk for being a smartaleck when he is asked where the toothpicks are located. But the average shopper doesn't pull out a gun and commit murder to put him in his place. This would be an extreme reaction.

There's a great gulf of gray between feeling angry at a boss who says, "You're a poor technical writer. These reports are unreadable," and resigning your job.

There's a great gulf of gray between feeling unloved by a spouse who says, "Are you going to find time to clean the house sometime this year?" and walking out of a marriage.

There's a great gulf of gray between feeling jealous when a coworker brags, "Just closed another deal. That puts me past the $1 million mark," and withholding information about the contract that will cause the newfound customer to nix the sale.

But we do encounter women who let their emotions run rampant. We had such an administrative assistant in our office a few years ago. One morning I was digging through the files for something — sitting in the middle of the floor and quite noticeable. Karra banged the back door as she entered the building and stalked right past me as I said, "Good morning." She kept her head down and never responded. Granted, she already had a reputation around the office for being "moody," but this was rather extreme behavior even for her. After all, I did sign her paycheck.

Immediately, I began to rack my brain for what might be upsetting her. No, she didn't have to work late Friday afternoon. No, this wasn't a holiday that the rest of the world took off. No, she hadn't been counseled about any recent work problems. So what was the deal?

I finished shuffling through the files and sauntered over to her cubicle. 'Good morning, Karra." She glared at me from the phone and never answered. The problem? I was truly perplexed. It was as if she'd become mute. Then a few minutes later I heard her talking to our travel agent in an irate tone of voice. It seems her college-age daughter had been flying to see a friend over the weekend, had gotten stranded in Oklahoma City, and the travel agent hadn't returned her phone call to her 800 number. So this was why she wasn't speaking to the rest of us in the office.

A few days later I phoned into the office from a client site to pick up my phone messages. I could tell from the sound of "Booher Consultants. This is Karra. How may I help you?" that something was terribly wrong. When I probed, I discovered that her teenage son had wrecked her car the night before and had no insurance. The impact of the event once again turned up in her tone. Such episodes continued until she finally lost her job.

Women who are victims of their moods will find it difficult to succeed on the job or in personal relationships.

Even with senior executives, emotions that simmer beneath the surface cause days like this: Jeri and her husband have a big argument about whether to go home for the holidays. As a parting shot at breakfast, he accuses, "You're thirty-six years old. How long are you going to keep letting your father tell you what to do?"

Three hours later, Jeri has a meeting with a colleague who wants her to terminate a nonproductive employee. With the husband's accusation still ringing in her ears, she refuses to hear the colleague out about his reasons, defends the poor performer, and determines to keep the employee on board against the other person's reservations.

Women who are victims of their moods will find it difficult to succeed on the job or in personal relationships.

Later in the day, Jeri's secretary tells her that she hadn't known where she was during the meeting and couldn't find her to take an important customer call. Jeri blows up at the secretary for being "overbearing and controlling." Then, just before she leaves for home, colleague Kevin sticks his head in her doorway and says in his blunt way, "Don't send that proposal out yet — I've got something that needs to be added." To which Jeri snaps, "I'll decide when the proposal goes out. And it's going out tomorrow whether we have your information or not."

Smart women who have mastered their moods would shake off the earlier argument with the husband. They would refuse to continue reacting to his comment throughout their day as they dealt with others and made decisions affecting other people.

Women who have mastered their emotions have a higher tolerance for frustration, use fewer put-downs, handle conflicts more effectively, avoid impulsive self-sabotaging reactions, reduce stress, and feel more positive about life. Daniel Goleman, in his best-selling book, *Emotional Intelligence,* cites study after study confirming the havoc emotions running amok play on our lives — at work and at home. He encourages us to be aware of our EQ (emotional quotient) as well as our IQ.

In fact, emotional decisions and gut reactions can be more than frustrating at work or home. They can cost money, waste time, and be downright dangerous.

If you don't master your moods, they'll muddle your mind.

Futurist Carolyn Corbin, founder of the Center for the 21st Century, tells about an emotional decision she made due to exhaustion from the travel demands of her career: "Actually, I was trying to avoid being on the road so much. I didn't sit down and logically think through why I wanted to start two new businesses, the service business and the retail business. I was just following my heart. I camouflaged the irrational part by doing all the logical things — like creating business plans and setting goals for both businesses. But when I really got down to it, I started those two businesses to avoid being on the road. Neither worked out like I intended."

Real-estate developer Vicky Weinberg tells about a time she was under a great deal of stress and had an emotional reaction that almost cost her a pile of money: "These prospective buyers had been traveling in and out of the country a lot, and I was under the gun to close the deal with them. My son was in the hospital, and it was a very emotional time for me. I just popped off to these people: 'You either close the deal today or you don't close it at all.' Later, my attorney said I had absolutely no right to say that according to the option clause in the contract. They could have carried on for another two or three years like that. But I just popped off under the predisposition of the moment."

Iris Torvik, Ph.D. and director of women's and infants'

If you don't master

your moods,

they'll muddle

your mind.

services at a large metropolitan hospital, says: "I've learned a lot about [emotions] and leadership, especially in dealing with physicians or large physician groups. I've learned to speak more from facts and logic, and not to present an issue unless I'm prepared to back it up with all the facts. I've learned that medicine is a predominately male environment, and they don't respond well to emotion. The same with administrators. It's very important to learn to be able to articulate correctly without throwing a lot of emotion into the equation."

Executive director of a nonprofit association, Terry Broomfield looks back on the emotion surrounding her decision to marry so soon after meeting her husband. Although it has been a successful marriage of many years, she says: "We met about two months after my husband's first wife had died, and we married about six months later. That was more emotional than rational. The whole process of marrying and parenting after being so independent and out in the working world was extremely different for me. We probably should have done more preparation. He was still suffering from what he had gone through with his wife, who had died after a prolonged illness. That was painful for him and, therefore, it was still painful for me. There was some real hurt and some problems along the way."

Susan Lanigan, associate general counsel with a national jewelry chain, says, "I'm very much an emotional decision maker. In everything from buying a house or a car to my career. The decision to leave the law firm and go with another was purely emotional. There was no logic involved in that, and that move didn't turn out well."

I'll have to add my own story to the above. Several years ago I was working on a writing project for a CEO of a large organization. He, several of his executives, and his wife, who headed up a division of the company, became bogged down about decisions affecting the project and several of their key clients who had a stake in the outcome. I felt caught in the middle of their internal squabbles, endless contradictions, and requests for rework on the project because "John doesn't want this," and "Sarah doesn't want that," and "Tom doesn't agree that we should include this."

One afternoon when he called with his latest request, I heard myself say, "I really don't have time to keep making these changes. I'd just like to withdraw from the whole project. You don't owe me a thing."

"What?" He sounded startled.

"If you're not pleased with the job we're doing, you don't owe me a thing."

"No, no, it's not that at all." He began to back-pedal, explaining that he and his staff couldn't agree on the details and that the issue was rife with internal politics. Thank goodness he insisted that I finish the project; otherwise, I would have lost a $50,000 project that I had spent three months to complete. It was an emotional comment that I'm glad I didn't have to live with!

So why *do* we let emotions sap our energy, mess up our moods, distract us from our work goals, and jeopardize our relationships?

Reason #1: Being Overworked and Overwhelmed

Work can be seductive. Smart women usually work at jobs they love. In addition to the feeling of satisfaction from work, successful women become seduced by recognition, respect, and rewards. Before they know it, they are caught up in the excitement and challenges. A job applicant not long ago sat in my office, explaining her reason for a job change:

"I know this sounds bad to be telling a prospective employer, but it's the truth. The job I now have requires my total waking hours. I'm responsible for recruiting, hiring, and training all the staff in all our stores nationwide, and they're retail people. That means they're open seven days a week. Of course, each store manager takes a day off, say every Tuesday, but I don't have a day off. On Saturday or Sunday they're open, so they're calling me with problems and issues to be resolved. When that manager takes his Tuesday off, I'm working with another manager who works Tuesday. I've done this for three years. At first it was exhilarating — such fast growth and big profits. They pay me very, very well. And the senior executives think I walk on water — getting those people hired and trained so fast. But it's been three years, it hasn't let up, and it's likely not going to." She paused and looked at me intently. "I want my life back."

Sometimes just the opposite is true. Work that's unpleasant can also overwhelm us, distract us, and muddy our moods. A joyless job can make us feel disappointed and defeated. It can wake us up at 3:00 a.m. with reminders about a brewing crisis that must be contained before noon.

Work — enjoyable and rewarding, or boring and disturbing — can be addictive. We work because it's a long-life pattern that we don't know how to control or because we don't know what else to do with our time. In either case — an exciting or boring job — our related emotions can make us feel overpowered, overwhelmed, and out of balance. Burnout results. Burnout occurs when we have too much to do, too little time to do it, over too long a period of time, with too little change-of-pace to release the pressure.

Work — enjoyable and rewarding, or boring and disturbing — can be addictive.

We blow, we burn, we crash.

This overwhelmed and out-of-control feeling pops up in every industry. In a recent issue of *The Washington Lawyer* (February 1997), writer Marilyn Tucker points out that only a few short years ago, a woman's primary complaint about the legal profession involved lack of career opportunity. Today the strongest dissatisfaction stems from pressures having to do with time and control, from balancing personal life and work life. This situation has surfaced as the number one issue in studies done by the bar associations, special task forces within companies, and alumnae associations. In one study done by the California Women Lawyers group, 92 percent of the respondents cited their biggest problem to be the balancing act.

Yes, some of us have helpful husbands. I fall into this lucky group. When I remarried eight years ago to a man who had been divorced and alone for 17 years, I didn't expect such a treasure chest of helpful habits and thoughtful gestures. He takes and retrieves my clothes from the dry cleaners. He stops by the store for fruit and milk. He keeps my car full of gas and handles the regular maintenance. He sorts the laundry. He buys greeting cards for family birthdays and events. He repots my plants when I let them die every season.

Some of us even have understanding bosses, or we're the understanding boss keeping our own staff afloat. And some of us were born with boundless energy. We've gone to all the time-management seminars and read all the books to become efficient, effective, and empowered at work. We meet, greet, hire, train, supervise, negotiate, document, sell, buy, write, motivate, and lead. Then we rush home and do the same things.

Despite helpful husbands and understanding bosses, the load can still be overwhelming.

Smart women know when to take a breather.

Women still carry the lion's share of the load at home. Despite help from others in the family, we still bear the burden of planning a couple's social calendar, tutoring kids through homework, shopping for the birthday gifts, remembering where the receipt is for the malfunctioning microwave, persuading the baseball coach to let Johnny try second base, writing the note to Joanna's teacher about her temperature, and transferring grandmother's x-rays to the right hospital.

Smart women know when to take a breather. They know when and how to say no. Unfortunately, they have to keep practicing the "no" message, because it goes against our giving nature. Even though I'm in the middle of writing this book and am on a very tight deadline, I still struggle with the concept. A colleague phoned last week to ask if I'd consider heading up an effort to put together a two-day educational seminar on authorship. His appeal proved strongly persuasive, because I do believe in giving back. I do enjoy talking about the writing life, but the laundry list of reasons dictating a no looked like this:

- Moving into our new building over the weekend and tying up all the loose ends, including malfunctioning technology,

- Having 40 days already committed to clients during the next three months,
  - Hiring and training a new graphic designer,
  - Motivating the sales reps to tackle a new territory with public workshops,
  - Writing a 60,000-word book,
  - Developing a proposal for another book my agent had already promised,
  - Helping my daughter with her newborn,
  - Developing a couples communication class for new second-marriage couples, and
  - Going for medical tests and treatment for an as-yet-undiagnosed problem.

Did I find it *easy* to say no to my colleague? No. Did I find it *necessary* to my sanity to say no to my colleague? Yes.

Women who are mastered by their moods waiver. One day they feel good and say yes; the next day they feel bad and say no — with a scowl and a negative attitude. Feeling pushed to the limit and finally understanding that a no to somebody's request is our only hope of survival, we often say that no with rage. With a snarl in our voice, gritted teeth, and a laundry list of explanations, our no sounds like an attack on the other person, simply because they ventured to ask us.

But smart women learn to say their no's with grace rather than gravel.

But smart women learn to say their no's with grace rather than gravel. They communicate their no's in a direct, controlled manner, starting with positives about the situation or request. They say no cheerfully, offering a brief explanation that's firm, and ending with aggressive suggestions as alternatives to accomplish the goal.

Smart women know when the tank is empty and stop to refuel before they have nothing but fumes left for the trip ahead.

Reason #2: Trying To Hang on to a Swinging Pendulum of Power

Sometimes women get caught with one hand on a

swinging pendulum. Our fear of being labeled "too emotional" or irrational pushes us too far in the other direction. We stifle our natural instincts and gut reactions, which in most cases would serve us well.

Ann-Marie Stephens, MBA director of technology and one of the few women of executive rank at her Fortune 500 company, explains it this way: "I'm in a meeting. I'm thinking, *I'm new to this culture; it's a new experience; I don't know all the players.* Then somebody says something and my emotional reaction is to just jump in and say, 'That's really nonsense.' But instead, I try to use logic, wait a minute, and remind myself, *You don't know all the players. You don't have all the information.* I stifle my instinctive response and wait — and that's hurt me quite a bit. I think if I would just say what I'm feeling at the time, I would probably be better off in the short run. Women want to be seen as logical and not emotional, but there are situations where, if you stifle your instinctive reaction too much, you miss the opportunity to have your greatest impact. What I've been learning is how to judge between the two."

Ann-Marie has grabbed the pendulum hindering many working women. She echoes the real dilemma — struggling with what you think or feel and running that through a set of filters, sometimes negative, about what others will think, what others expect, and what the culture dictates. In other words, we think about how we *should* think and feel instead of being honest and forthright.

Entrepreneur Amy Quigley Rudy, president of ModelOffice, a fast-growing software development company, tells about trying to go with the gut — against her people: "When I was younger I worked all on emotion. I would go with the gut and do what my instincts told me. I made a lot of mistakes, but for the most part, I always felt I was doing the right thing. So I always had passion about what I was doing. Then I found I had stepped on some people's toes. Because I felt very, very sure and even righteous about what I'd decided, I defended my position to the end. That can have some real adverse effects. I had several people tell me, 'You know, you

We stifle our natural instincts and gut reactions, which in most cases would serve us well.

need to back off.'

"Then I overcompensated until I got to the point where I was overanalyzing everything. I'd say, 'Let me bring another person in.' Before I knew it, I had done nothing and had turned down a lot of opportunities to even make a mistake. Now I feel like I'm centered. I'm more able to tackle both the left side and the right side of the brain and come up with the best decision."

Thoughts generate emotions. Negative thoughts generate negative emotions, like worrying about things that may never happen, telling yourself that you may fail on an upcoming task, or reasoning with yourself that he didn't call about the weekend because you're a boring person. None of these uplift, motivate, or encourage.

Negative thoughts produce nasty moods, which will keep you from being who you want to be and accomplishing what you want to accomplish. Part of changing the way you feel is capturing the thoughts that got you there. By training yourself to think positive thoughts and driving out the negatives, you feel at ease when forced to make those tough decisions.

Reason #3: Letting Others Yank You Around and Pull You Down

Too many people have let others chart their emotional course. Someone else pulls the string and they laugh, cry, live, and love on cue.

Actress turned corporate trainer, Chris Casady, talks about living by everybody else's rules: "My parents instilled in me that I should try to please other people. My own opinions as a child were never valued. It was more like, 'These are the rules, and this is what you need to do.' As long as I was happy and upbeat, they liked to be around me. So I just tried to do what they wanted me to do and was hopeful that was going to get me by."

A training consultant and manager tells about a five-year period of her life while her children were in junior and senior high when she had a relationship with an attorney who was an alcoholic: "I can remember allowing him not only to be verbally abusive to me, but to them. I will feel guilty forever, even though I have worked through some of it. My guilt stems from not drawing boundaries, not only for myself, but for my children, who were dependent on me to do that for them."

Guilt weighs us down.

A boss's reaction to a long-term illness took another smart woman by surprise: "Just out of the blue, I began to have physical problems. I lost lots of weight and had to be off work quite awhile. I was in intensive care of the hospital for nine days, then back to work half days and so forth. But what I couldn't believe was my boss's *reaction* to it. When I couldn't generate the expected revenue through billable hours, he wanted me out. He started building his case to have me fired. I was just so puzzled and upset — floored by the way he treated me because of the situation. Finally, I understood that it was not about me. I had to decide to do as much work as I could do, but not get into a mood where I was letting him beat me up over something I couldn't help."

Guilt weighs

us down.

Public school teacher Nancy Koenig recalls a college roommate who pulled her chain: "She had been my debate partner all of my older teenage years and had contributed to my feelings about myself. I was 5'8" and she was only 4'11". Tiny. Always had boyfriends. But when she went off to school with me, she was pregnant and unmarried. I was the only one who knew, and I was supposed to keep her secret. She was depressed and worried, and I felt very put upon. It was a big load to have her so dependent on me through all that. I thought, *I've had to deal with her all these years, and now I've got to be the only one to help her!* It was like she was an assignment I'd been given."

Jeanine Brannon, a management consultant practicing in West Palm Beach, Florida, explains a family turmoil that took its toll on her emotions: "My father died two years ago and it was always understood that I would administrate the estate. Mother really looked to me to help her. But I started getting all kinds of pressures from the family to do things I didn't agree with. One would call to tell me to pressure mother to sell something and the next week another family member would call me to reverse it. I gave up rather than work through it. I just threw in the towel."

Parenting puts us in a whole new predicament — allowing people to push and pull and tug at our emotions. Gay Knight, a project manager at a Fortune 50 company, explains: "My son made a D in chemistry, even though he has been labeled 'gifted' and has been in gifted honor programs throughout school. I became very angry over it and couldn't understand where he was coming from, so I quickly pulled him out of his other plans and made him go through summer school. It caused some problems in our relationship, I think, because of the anger and the abruptness with which I handled it. Looking back on it, I still think it was the right thing for him, but I probably should have approached it differently to avoid damaging our relationship."

Another thing women battle: We get our feelings hurt when we should get angry. And when we're hurt, we sometimes yell, blame, accuse, and counterattack. Our reaction can often damage a relationship.

An attorney confides about her silent suffering and the resentment it created: "For a long time, I resented my husband. I blamed him for having to go to work full time and be away from the children. I was very angry at him, but I lacked the appropriate conflict resolution skills to deal with it. So I would just keep it inside. Finally, I reached a point where I had to decide if I was going to destroy the marriage because of this or work at a marriage I really wanted. Once I made the decision to get over it and go on, that was all it took. I realized that this was going to destroy the very thing I wanted to hold on to."

Often we suffer in silence. We never let the other person know they hurt our feelings, so their behavior never changes. We nurse the grudge until it becomes a festering sore. We tend to just bite our tongue and reason "What good would it do?" or "If I mention it, it'll just make things worse."

Before long, the frustration caused by others seeps out in

Once I made the decision to get over it and go on, that was all it took.

hurtful ways. When a woman's life becomes miserable because a child won't apply himself in school, a teen won't stop driving recklessly, or an employee won't turn in his project reports on time, she gets to her wit's end and then explodes. She often resorts to sarcasm, subtle digs into the ego, or ridicule to shame the other person into shaping up.

But smart women speak up when something happens that hurts or frustrates them. They get the situation out in the open through a series of questions that allows the other person to explain, to interpret their intentions, and either to apologize or alter their words or behavior.

Rather than demotivate, smart women motivate others to correct their mistakes and improve their performance or behavior.

Rather than demotivate, smart women motivate others to correct their mistakes and improve their performance or behavior. They point out the issue or problem. They let the other person know they understand past efforts and other strengths. They describe the things that have to be changed specifically. They explain clearly the consequences of the other person's not changing the behavior or situation. Then they end on a positive note, expressing confidence that the other person will make the necessary improvements.

Like so many other things in life, mood management requires both determination and skill.

Reason #4: Inner Conflict in Your Life

Negative moods can be the visible output of inner turmoil. We deal with the same issue over and over and over. Feeling disappointed with yourself that you didn't finish college. Feeling unloved because your older brother won more of your dad's time. Feeling unattractive because you've gained weight. Feeling resentment that your spouse never acknowledges your work achievements. Feeling angry that your alcoholic sister can't hold a job. Feeling guilty that your baby died when you turned your back. Feeling embarrassed that a child chose a life of drugs. Feeling responsible that a parent died alone.

I lived with such inner turmoil for almost twenty years in my first marriage. My husband suffered from extremely low self-esteem and depression due to years of emotional abuse as a child. Early in our marriage, before I learned that such a task was impossible, I began a crusade to build his self-esteem and talk him out of depression. Although an excellent listener and encourager to others, he could not help himself. For years, I tried to cover for his bouts of depression that began to affect his job and relationships by making excuses for all the symptoms. Despite years of on-and-off therapy with various psychologists and psychiatrists, he grew worse and worse. The doctors tested, advised, medicated, and counseled, but nothing helped.

What to do, what to do, what to do? It was like a fire raging out of control in my mind, day after day. Finally, at my threat of leaving him unless he got further help and followed through on his therapists' suggestions, he committed himself to a hospital. On medication, he improved for a short period, and then quickly relapsed to the same state. He refused to return to the hospital or to hold a job. He talked repeatedly of suicide and withdrew into his own world.

Every day I struggled by myself to keep the household running, to endure my sadness over being virtually alone in the relationship, to agonize over having him committed against his will, and to struggle with my commitment to remain married "for better or worse" amidst the demands of daily life in such a situation.

At times, I felt like a split personality, cheery and upbeat in front of a client or an audience, and despairing at home. Only after I made the decision to divorce my husband to save my own sanity did I understand what a toll the turmoil had taken on my own spirit and health.

When the drain of having to "put on a happy face" every day for my kids, my audiences, and the rest of the world stopped, life felt better. When the pain of feeling totally responsible for my husband stopped, life felt good once again.

Conflict that bubbles under the surface boils over from time to time when some person or circumstance turns the heat up in our lives. A boss who criticizes curtly generates a pout rather than corrective action. A two-year-old who wets the bed produces fear that he won't be able to hold a job at age 27. A headstrong teen with a penchant for smarting off to teachers triggers resentment meant for our domineering father.

Such conflict reflected in our mood swings hardens over a long period of time. Speaker and management consultant Dru Scott Decker, Ph.D., who often works with senior executives at client firms, agrees: "Usually the thing I find when I work with people is that it's not some new problem that just drops on them like a boulder out of the sky. It's the same old problem that they've let grow and grow and grow, and it finally overtakes them."

Unresolved conflict forms the foundation of our emotional terrain. When someone steps in it before the cement hardens and takes shape, they leave a footprint. That footprint of emotion is usually visible to everyone.

Smart women listen to good friends and family members who see the pattern, lovingly point it out, and encourage them to resolve the issues before they cause destruction in their lives.

Reason #5: Physical Failures

Yes, there are physical reasons for mood swings: PMS, nutritional deficiencies, sleep deprivation, chemical imbalances, and malfunctioning organs. Some of the physical conditions are brought on by the causes mentioned above. Others invade our world from out of nowhere. After you've ruled out other causes under your own control, check out the physical and do what is necessary to bring what is out of balance into balance.

Gaining Mastery Over the Moods

Find out what's eating you inside. Most of us know

already. Terry Broomfield reflects on her childhood: "The biggest inner turmoil in my life is that I had a brother fourteen months younger than I was, and there was tremendous jealousy and conflict between the two of us. While we grew up and respected each other, that was never really resolved, which was a shame. I think we both held a lot of rage inside about the other."

There comes a time when rage must run into resolution. An organizational development consultant explains how she quickly came to terms with a major mistake made early in life. She married a man who was mentally ill and couldn't hold a job: "After two-and-a-half years we had moved fourteen times and he had had fourteen different jobs. With every move, I was trying to convince employers that it wasn't me, that it was my husband. I realized that in order for me to have any kind of stable life, I had to move on. I think I blamed my mother up until the time I made the decision to divorce. My home life was good, but it was just that my mother owned her own business, I worked in her business, and she expected a lot. I was not paid for it — other than they were sending me to school. I think I just became infatuated with somebody older than I. He'd been to medical school, and I thought he was going to be the answer to all my problems. Little did I know that he was the beginning of the problem.

There comes

a time when

rage must run

into resolution.

"But once I made the decision to leave the marriage, I stopped blaming my mother. I just realized that it was my life. I had to say to myself: 'I can't believe I did that. I can't believe I made a major decision like that. And I'm now responsible. I'm in the driver's seat of my life. I have to accept responsibility for whatever happens and I must go forward.' Once I came to that realization, I had a very clear goal, and I laid out my objectives and plans to get there."

Replace Blame With Awareness

Instead of blaming others for how they've shaped our attitudes or lives and the accompanying emotions and moods, consider what has happened to *them* that made them the way they are. What were *their* parents like? What was *their* culture? What was *their* struggle? What worried *them* half to death? How did *they* learn to talk to themselves to cope and survive?

For years, I blamed my ex-husband's father for the emotional abuse that ruined his son's life and eventually our marriage. When my ex would be in a communicative mood (and it was rare that he would talk about his past) he would relive some of the conversations and situations of his childhood. Rage would well up inside me. Driving to work in tears, I'd catch myself gritting my teeth and muttering into the silence, "Why, why, why did you do this to him? How could you ruin our lives? The kids will have to go through the pain of seeing us split up, all because of you!"

But as I talked with other members of his family and learned about the hard life his father had experienced as a child, being abandoned by his own parents, I came to understand. He'd had only a few years of schooling before he was forced to drop out of grade school to work the cotton fields to put his older brothers and sisters through school. They were supposed to have helped send him back to school, but that never happened. Without an education, he was doomed to poverty that destroyed his own self-esteem.

When he finally did find a way to make a living, he attributed that modicum of success to the fact that he "fought back." As a parent, he wrongly assumed that if he denigrated and ridiculed his son, the son would fight back also and make something of himself. His intentions were good; his methods were wrong.

Understanding his beginnings and motivations finally allowed me to forgive my ex-father-in-law for the damage he'd done to his son and ultimately to our family.

That is not to say that understanding why people are like they are will change them. It simply means that as we become aware, we grow more tolerant. As we grow more tolerant, the more distance we can put between the conflict and emotions and actions triggered by the situation or person.

Debbie Hertzog, specialist on children with learning disabilities and mother of two vivacious boys, explains her emotional stability this way: "I'm really happy with myself, and I like myself. That was resolved years ago. I have a strong spiritual belief about who I am. Basically, I'm just really happy and healthy, so I can then be free to share myself with others. I really, really like other people."

Debbie shows unusual perceptivity about how inner conflict saps energy and drives emotions — and eventually diminishes the gift of ourselves we have to present to others.

Replace Resentment With Gratitude

Another smart mother has explored her deep resentment of her husband and has learned to master the emotion with gratitude: "I became very resentful of my husband because he was a teacher. He made only $30-35,000 a year, and in my mind that meant I'd have to be the primary breadwinner. I couldn't go part-time. I couldn't even really change my law career at all. I was very, very resentful because he had more time with the kids — home at 4:00, holidays off. I made him feel really terrible. All my friends said, 'Hey, you're so lucky.' But I didn't feel I had a choice at all. The rational side of me always knew I had a saint of a husband, who did it all. He kept the house clean. He did the grocery shopping. He worked really hard, and he was very, very good at a lot more important work than what I did. But I was just so bitter about it.

You just have to learn the lesson and keep repeating the lesson: You have choices.

"Then I had this very close friend, who is very perceptive, point out how really lucky I was and that I did have choices. Granted, I might not have the choice to sit home and eat bon-bons, but I did have choices other than a law career. So I made some changes in my life. I learned to appreciate my husband. Finally, it sunk in. You just have to learn the lesson and keep repeating the lesson: You have choices. I now have a good life and a good marriage."

Instead of rolling resentment into bed with you at night, grab gratitude. Smart women focus on what's right in their lives. Do you have a roof over your head? Do you have good health? Do you earn a paycheck? Do you have capable mental capacity? Do you have a meaningful job? Do you have a friend who loves you? Do you have a supportive family? Do you have a child who gives you joy? Do you have something to look forward to next month?

Jennifer Raymond, technical manager at a Fortune 500 company, feels gratitude when she thinks about the lives of older women in her family: "My great grandmother crossed Texas and went into Oklahoma in a wagon. She gave birth in a dugout. She had to put her kids' crib legs in candle water to keep the fleas off. She bore four children in that environment — and there's no way to know how many she lost to miscarriages. Seven years after they got there, they had money to build a structure — so they bought the barn because the animals needed it. It was fifteen years before she had a house. When they first started welfare, the county elected her to go around and decide who needed help. After a week of her traveling the county, she came back and resigned — because there was no one in the county she'd met who was working any harder and living any poorer than she was.

"When I look at my dishwasher and my washing machine, I think we're so blessed. We don't have to worry about food — just whether we cook in or eat out. I don't have to worry if we're going to be able to go the doctor. My mother, when I was fifteen, quit doing business at a bank because they wouldn't let her buy a car without her husband cosigning. I feel incredibly lucky to have come into history when I can acquire the skills I need and use those skills to succeed. There's just no place for pity — beating yourself up over what somebody else has got over on the other side of town."

Iris Torvik says, "I do motivational things. What I love to do is make rounds in the patient-care areas and get down to the heart of my front-line people: the patients and the staff. There's a manager between me and the staff, so just coming in at odd times during the day or night and sitting at a nursing station to talk with them gives me a real good perspective on why I'm here. I get a lot of energy from that."

Katy Crane, vice president of new product development at Core Media, says, "I have energy because I'm thankful. I'm satisfied. I'm not worried or frightened. You know all those emotions that just zap the heck out of you? I'm not filled with those. I'm basically thankful."

Smart women focus on gratitude. Then they have less time to let resentment root in their psyche.

Replace Guilt With Permission

Life is full of tragedies that produce guilt. Former lawyer and now stay-at-home mom, Laurie Barringer says: "My biggest struggle was letting go of my dependence on mom and dad. I had a brother who died when he was sixteen. He was two years older than I, and when that happened, all the focus turned on me. I was under a microscope. I felt like I had to meet their expectations, and I was supposed to be my mom's best friend all my life, always staying near her side. It was always on my mind. I still call her a lot — we talk three or four times a week. It's still a struggle to let her know that I've grown up, gotten married, and I haven't forgotten her. I'll always feel the need to be there for her. But it was really hard to break away." Laurie finally gave herself permission to live her own life.

Smart women focus

on gratitude.

Terry Broomfield goes on to explain how she came to awareness and final resolution with the inner turmoil regarding her brother and mother. "She [Mother] had a tough time herself. I think probably my brother was unexpected. There was seven years difference between my older brother and me, and I was born during the late twenties. My father was a stockbroker, and we lost everything we had. So she was not only dealing with two little kids, but the loss of two houses and just about everything. She didn't do anything hurtful to me on purpose. I just didn't feel that I got the attention I wanted. But she had to deal with major things going on her life — things happening to her family because we were penniless. I finally realized all this and stopped blaming her. She was a good woman and she did the best she could under the circumstances."

Terry understands what guilt can do and undo. There is wisdom in her reflections. Guilt can weigh us down. Guilt can sap our energy. Guilt can make us physically sick. Guilt can stop forward progress in our career. Guilt can end a relationship. Guilt can suck the spirit from our life.

Guilt is something Angie Casey, a mother of two whose systems analyst job requires that she often work 10- to 12-hour days, understands: "There is turmoil in raising kids with our hectic schedule. I've really not been as active in church as when I was growing up, so the kids are not participating in choirs and some of those things. This year when the children's choir sang, my kids were not singing — although they have in the past. So I feel I've missed out on the opportunities for the oohs and aahs this year."

Smart women give themselves permission to be less than perfect.

Smart women give themselves permission to be less than perfect.

If your emotional upheaval comes from guilt over things done or left undone, give yourself permission to make some mistakes. In fact, give yourself permission to make some whopping mistakes. Most great people can count many mistakes in their past — and then count them as learning experiences that will serve them well later. Smart women own up to past foolish choices and give themselves permission to profit from them and move on.

Get Centered

Smart women find their center — their core, the inner calm that helps them deflect attacks and resist seductions from the outside. Of those interviewed, 69 percent mentioned the importance of prayer or meditation and 97 percent mentioned time alone to replenish their spirit and refocus their thinking.

Smart women own up to past foolish choices and give themselves permission to profit from them and move on.

Lisa Porterfield, organizational development specialist, says, "Reading new books and learning new information really pumps me up. The more I know, the more confident and competent I can be. And there's a kind of energy that comes from feeling accepted and valued."

All but a few of the smart women interviewed also mentioned their dedication to staying mentally and physically healthy by eating right and exercising. (Unfortunately, resting didn't surface in the conversations nearly enough!)

According to the Surgeon General's "Physical Activity and Health Report" released in July 1996, fewer than 40 percent of the adults in the US get the recommended amount of 30 minutes or more of moderate physical exercise daily. Regular physical exercise can combat stress and depression. In short, it makes you feel good.

Eating right can have the same effect. Eat fresh raw fruits and vegetables and more complex carbohydrates, increase fiber, drink plenty of liquids, don't skip meals, reduce fats, reduce salt, ,reduce sugar, cut caffeine, and take vitamins and nutrients to supplement your diet.

Rest! Find out how many hours of sleep you need to make you feel refreshed in the morning. Then sleep that much — every night.

Smart women have learned to connect their body with their emotions. They know what makes them feel calm, collected, and confident.

Smart women have learned to connect their body with their emotions.

Here are other suggestions from smart women:

- Get rid of the clutter.
- Simplify your routines.
- Be realistic about what you can do in any given day.
- Realize that everything takes longer than you think.
- Read good books.
- Listen to relaxing music.
- Spend time on a hobby — something you really enjoy.
- Exercise: walk, swim, cycle, ski, garden, shop.
- Keep your sense of humor.
- Pamper yourself with warm baths.
- Rest (forget work) one day a week.
- Take periodic vacations and retreats with others or alone.
- Pay for conveniences, the things you don't enjoy doing for yourself.
- Do for yourself the things you enjoy, even if paying for such services "makes more sense."
- Live within your means, making sure you can afford what you buy.
- Give up your expectations about what others should do,

be, and say.

- Create comfortable surroundings.
- Keep things in your plans that you can look forward to.
- Get regular physical checkups.
- Appreciate and enjoy nature.
- Spend time with little kids full of wonder.
- Network with other women with whom you can bounce off ideas regarding your career and personal situations.
- Reconnect with your friends.
- Stay away from negative people.
- Continuously learn new things.
- Believe in the future.

A friend once summed up this way: "I have the tendency to act — and then backstroke. Many of these actions come from my emotions."

Smart women master their moods.

2
Seek a Sense of
Self-Worth

W hy is self-esteem so crucial to success? Because your sense of self and the picture of yourself that you create for the world affects every major decision of your life: marriage partner, career, friends, faith, leisure, and lifestyle. Your self-concept affects your attitudes and reactions, your behavior and your thoughts, your happiness or unhappiness.

It's no secret that many women suffer from low self-esteem. Psychologists pinpoint low self-esteem as the basis for teen pregnancies and promiscuity, for staying in abusive marital relationships, and for enduring excessive conflict on the job. If its presence contributes so strongly to success and its absence wreaks such havoc, you'd think people would be more attentive to finding its source. Not so. Ask women about their first memories of feeling a success or failure and most will have to give it careful thought.

Smart women make sure their success rests on pillars rather than platforms.

Some women build their self-concept on a single "platform" or role they play in life: daughter of..., wife of..., mother of..., or employee/employer of.... Then, when one of these platforms crumbles through divorce, death, or downsizing, so does their sense of self and ultimately their outlook on life.

Smart women make sure their success rests on pillars rather than platforms.

To hold themselves up during these tough times, smart

women build strong, multiple pillars of self-esteem: multiple sources of relationships, activities, and accomplishments that support them. When their children disappoint them, they still feel valued as a spouse and an employee or employer. When their marriage runs into temporary or permanent difficulties, they gain strength from accomplishments at work or in the community. And when work disappoints them, they can draw on their friendships, mothering, or wifely roles for satisfaction and a sense of value.

Smart women seek a sense of self-worth and demonstrate self-confidence to others by thinking pillars rather than platforms.

Self-Esteem Damaged by Childhood Haunts

...smart women build strong, multiple pillars of self-esteem: multiple sources of relationships, activities, and accomplishments that support them.

Some women have had a major wound inflicted on their psyche during childhood. No doubt, there are parents, teachers, and community volunteers who have had a large hand in building our prisons as well as our schools. They've created or perpetuated walls and bars that hold children captive well into their adult years.

An interviewee confides: "When I was at home, I pretty much lived in my own world. I escaped from my family — I read a lot. I did what I was told. My parents struggled to make ends meet. My mother got a degree when most women didn't. Here was an obviously bright woman who married my dad, the dreamer, who couldn't balance a checkbook and didn't think it was all that important anyway. It must have been pretty frantic for her. Her own disappointment and lack of self-esteem got mixed into the air where we grew up. I just never quite knew where she was coming from. I tried to please her, but nothing I tried ever did."

In recent studies of women suffering from anorexia and other eating disorders, researchers have discovered that children who didn't get hugged and cuddled in their childhood years became troubled adults. When teachers, parents, or peers reject children — intentionally or through neglect — those children come to doubt they have what it takes to make it in school and later in life.

Daniel Goleman, in his best-seller, *Emotional Intelligence,* makes the point this way: "Whether or not a child arrives at school on the first day of kindergarten with these capabilities depends greatly on how much her parents — and preschool teachers — have given her the kind of care that amounts to a "Heart Start," the emotional equivalent of the Head Start program.

Comments from another interviewee: "My dad was very hard to please. He found fault with just everything. If you said it was sunny, he was going to say it was cloudy. You could hear him take a cherished position on something — politics, the environment, anything. He was really pro big-business and hated all the 'tree-huggers.' And so, just for sport, you could take his side on the argument and then watch him take the new side — just to argue with you. Nothing I ever did was good enough for him. 'You should have done it this way or that way,' he'd say. It was usually after something turned out wrong. He didn't ever tell you ahead of time — just that you should have known it wouldn't work."

Another interviewee confides, "For me, it was my older brother. We were basically like twins, and when we started school, I skipped the first grade, so I was in the second grade with him. From then on we were in the same classes, same homeroom teacher, and all that. Unfortunately, I was the type of kid who basically wanted to please the teachers. I did extremely well in reading, writing, spelling, and that sort of thing. He didn't. So from early childhood days, there was this competition. He was very critical of me. Had it not been for my mother, I would have really been a mess because of his constant criticism. He'd say, 'You're not worth anything. You're only a girl. You're only going to grow up and get married.' "

Another respondent, although admitting her parents always encouraged her to do well, had this to say: "I still feel this compulsion — when I do something really well — to call and report in. I always feel compelled to report on my successes. It's not that they were ever negative. It's just that they were so neutral, so unemotional about everything. I always tried to get bigger and bigger accomplishments just to get a rise out of them, but I never could. I still never can."

The good news for those who have felt sagging self-esteem from time to time since childhood is that you now hold the key to such prison cells. You can let yourself walk out free.

Self-Esteem Damaged by a Demeaning Spouse or Boyfriend

Some women let significant others in their life control their own perception of themselves. Popular talk-show host, Dr. Laura Schlessinger, points out that dating should be about selecting, not about being selected. Women are so busy making sure that a man wants them, they fail to question whether they want the man. Making a man the judge and jury of your self-worth places a woman in a painful, dangerous spot. Dr. Schlessinger goes on to point out to a particular caller: "When you move in with a man without a commitment, he already knows one crucial thing: He doesn't have to do much to get you. Then he fools around, and you stay, and he learns something more: He doesn't have to do much to keep you, either. And that has to be crushing to your self-respect."

...you now hold

the key

to such

prison cells.

Far too many women place their sense of self-worth in the hands of a man who hasn't a clue what to do with it. So he drops it to the ground and stomps on it. Sometimes the damage is done with the tongue, sometimes with the fist.

"Until I knew that the doctor I was involved with for over five years was an alcoholic, I just thought there was something the matter with me. This was a person who was very intelligent, very good-looking, very well-to-do financially. I just thought, *Why can't I relate to him, get along with him? Why am I not enough for him?*"

An insurance executive, who is now divorced, explains emotional abuse during twenty-one years of marriage: "I don't think I'm the only person who's ever been through this, but you get trapped by someone else's negative thinking. On a constant basis I heard things like, 'You don't know. You don't understand things like this. This is all your fault.' It's easy to get trapped into believing those things from someone you love."

An engineer responding to the survey had this reflection about her own self-esteem journey: "I started demanding that I be treated with respect, but it required my deciding that I was worth it. As long as I was willing to accept the fundamental notion that there was something wrong with me, that I was to be shamed, then it continued. But when I refused to continue to be shamed, it stopped immediately."

Author and speaker, Judith Briles, Ph.D., writes in her book, *When God Says No,* about her struggle in such an earlier relationship: "When I married Steve, I knew that all the dreams, all the hopes, and all the fairy tales were true. But several years later, as I came tumbling down two flights of stairs — pushed down in a violent fit of rage by my husband — my dreams were shattered for the last time. All hope of happiness cracked with each thud of my body. Bloodied and bruised, beaten down emotionally and physically, I knew I had reached the end. I made my decision. This was it. I didn't care how stupid he thought I was. I didn't care how low he made me feel. Deep down inside I knew that no matter what kind of terrible person he had convinced me I was, I wasn't terrible or stupid or ugly enough to deserve this."

"I wasn't terrible or stupid or ugly enough to deserve this."

Judith picked herself up off the floor — literally and figuratively. The sad part is that some women don't.

Self-Esteem Damaged by a Temporary or Resident Critic in Your Life

Women can also be the frequent target, the convenient scapegoat, of the extended family or the workplace. They feel other people's fury for short bursts of time during their life. Bosses who are particularly inept at giving feedback about the job can injure self-esteem with callous comments, reminders of every past mistake, or character attacks. As a result, some women take the comments to heart and become believers, feeling paralyzed to make improvement.

One interviewee explained her reactions to a boss who

was stingy with praise: "My boss gives very minimal positive feedback, and it is very hard for me to read him. Whenever I do a presentation or report or anything, and I feel as though I put a lot of time and effort into it, it seems like he is always picking it apart. That really challenged me when I first started reporting to him. At first I had the feeling that it was never going to work. I felt very micro-managed."

Dora Grider, president of her own mortgage company, recalls a short stint working for someone else: "It was probably the only time in my life when I would go to work with a knot in my throat."

Another interviewee reflects on a coworker who created big gaping holes of doubt during a certain period of her life: "I couldn't do anything right for him. Even if there was a compliment that came my way from the news director or the producer, he'd add something like, 'Well, the story would *really* have been spectacular *if* it had run a week earlier.'"

Relatives that "come and go" in your life can also turn up the heat: "My mother-in-law used to live about five minutes away from me. She is a lovely person, but she and I do not get along," confides another interviewee, an attorney. "She loves her granddaughter, but she is crazy. She just doesn't like me as a person. I've had to build some pretty strong boundaries. I tried to limit my interaction with her, and eventually we had a parting of the ways. It was shortly after my cancer surgery. I decided that she was a very negative person — she exudes negative energy. I couldn't deal with it. I had to let her go. We meet only in neutral territory. The world is full of very positive, upbeat people, and I needed to be around those people."

> *When somebody knows you have to have everybody smiling at you, then you give them control over your life.*

When somebody knows you have to have everybody smiling at you, then you give them control over your life. You become their puppet, and they pull your strings. That's a difficult way to live for long periods of time, and it can cause tremendous damage to your self-esteem.

You will always be waiting for the compliment, and when it doesn't come, or a critical remark surfaces in its place again and again, your self-respect can vanish.

Regain Your Self-Respect Through Association With Winners

Whatever the reasons or sources for lack of self-esteem, the good news is that damage to self-respect can be repaired. You can look at yourself in the mirror and see a new you.

If you don't think much of yourself, consider what other people think of you. Take a close look at the people around you — your spouse, your friends, your colleagues, and your customers or clients. Are they intelligent people? Are they kind people? Are they creative? Are they honest? If so, why not try trusting their judgment about you? Would they choose a worthless person to marry, to befriend, to buy from, to work with?

Attitude is contagious. If you don't believe it, just place a recorder in the center of the lunch table tomorrow. If someone complains about a new policy, others tend to follow suit and focus on the negative side. If someone shows delight over an upcoming holiday, everyone typically chimes in.

If your self-esteem needs bolstering, associate more closely with people you admire. Become observant of their attitudes and actions that reflect self-confidence: How do they dress and carry themselves? How do they react to compliments from others? How do they handle their successes? How do they accept responsibility for mistakes? How do they handle setbacks?

Attitude is contagious.

You can build your own confidence by associating with and modeling others who are confident — through both defeats and victories.

Regain Your Self-Respect Through Your Own Accomplishments

Because their father had had such a difficult time with low self-esteem, I was determined to build a strong sense of self in my children early on. One day when I picked up my daughter, Lisa, from kindergarten, she jumped in the front seat and stuck out her artwork for me to see. "My teacher said it was the best one in the class." I commented appropriately at that assessment.

She continued, "See how I colored in the lines. And I'm also good at printing my name." She began to rock back and forth on her heels against the back of the front seat, beaming her smile down on me as I sat behind the wheel. "And I'm also good at printing my numbers. Look over on the back. And I'm also good at running. I outran all the boys in my class at recess. And I'm also good at —" She stopped and looked at me as smugly as any five-year-old can: "I can't think of anything I'm not good at."

I didn't want to burst her bubble. I knew the world would work to do that soon enough.

Accomplished women often owe their confidence to a mother's nudges and nurturing. Dr. Sallie T. Hightower, a senior manager at a large oil-and-gas company, attributes her accomplishments to a mother with strong influence: "She was a feminist before her time. She had four kids — me and three brothers. But she always protected me when they tried to run over me. She helped me hold my own with them at the dinner table. She listened to what I had to say and would make the others listen to me, too. She instilled confidence in me about what I could do. She always told me there were no limitations on my potential. Mother didn't have an education or a career for herself, but she valued those things. She told me I could have them."

Reliving your accomplishments can be like a dose of good medicine.

Dr. Carolyn Corbin had the same kind of nurturing: "We never had a lot of money, but Dad always said, 'If you want to go to Harvard, I'll get you there.' I don't know how they did it, but they always led me to believe that whatever I wanted to do, some way, somehow, all the aunts and uncles would pool their money and get me there. I felt very important as a child."

Reliving your accomplishments can be like a dose of good medicine. A middle manager at IBM puts it this way: "My husband says, 'You always do well. Why do you get so worked up and nervous about things?' I've finally realized that it's just part of my makeup — that's part of how I get ready for things — by thinking through all the bad things that could happen to me and all the things that I could mess up, and then planning for them so they don't happen.

"What I try to do is look back at things that people have said about me. In fact, at work I used to keep this little praise folder — a little manila folder where I kept all the notes that people had sent me — 'Congratulations' or 'wow' about some great thing I had pulled off. I just tucked those away and sometimes when I'm feeling that nothing good has been going on, I pull those out. It makes me feel better to see all of those things that I've accomplished. Sometimes just writing your resume helps you feel like you've accomplished a lot of things."

By accomplishment, I don't necessarily mean a job or a career.

Kathleen Wu, an attorney in Dallas, says, "You get more from work than the financial. It's the inner satisfaction and sense of self-esteem. I see this with so many young women lawyers who crave that satisfaction. They've been working maybe three or four years, then quit to stay home. And once they give that up, they say it's hard to rebuild it in other areas of their lives."

By accomplishment, I don't necessarily mean a job or a career

What Kathleen alludes to here is not necessarily a paycheck, but the feeling of accomplishment. The feeling of planting part of yourself and watching it grow to maturity, a tangible outcome. There's nothing that will build your self-esteem like seeing a project through from planning to completion: A creative photo album you've assembled, a gourmet meal, a house redecorated, a book written and published, a solo sung, a theater character created and applauded, a convention planned and executed, a bridge built across the bay, an entrepreneurial company organized, grown, and sold.

Regain Your Self-Respect by Earning Money

As a child and later a teenager, my daughter, Lisa, always joked about her lack of enough allowance to get her through the week and her long Christmas wish list. When I'd comment on her spending habits, she would say, "I'm going to grow up and marry a rich doctor." I'd correct her, "No, you need to grow up and *be* a rich doctor to support your tastes."

Please hear me straight on this issue: I don't equate earning money with value as a person. Many very smart women have never entered the workforce and have never earned a dime from an employer for their hard work.

My point here, however, is that for some women, earning their own money — and the freedom that provides — bolsters their self-esteem. A senior executive responding to the survey sums it up this way: "Because I was overweight somewhat, I think I always gravitated toward getting really, really good grades and excelling academically. I've finally got enough in the bank that it [my weight] doesn't matter anymore."

If you're one of these women, and circumstances have been altered so that you're no longer bringing home a paycheck, you may simply need to become aware of what has punctured a hole in your confidence balloon and to see how you might plug the leak in other ways.

I don't equate

earning money

with value

as a person.

Regain Your Self-Respect Through Your "Packaging"

How much is your self-esteem tied to your appearance? One of the interviewees, a very beautiful woman herself, put it this way: "There was a time when everything was going wrong in life. I didn't exercise, and my diet was lousy. So I stepped back and said, 'I don't like myself anymore.' It's like when you turn forty and everything gets stuck in a handbag, along with gravity and your body. I have friends who're so miserable because they don't take time for themselves."

When asked, "How much do you think physical attractiveness still matters in our culture?" 100 percent of the women I surveyed answered, "A lot!"

The vast majority of the respondents went on to recall situations in which women were undeservedly rewarded because of good looks or unnecessarily penalized or minimized because of their looks. Although they said that a man's appearance also colored others' perception of his abilities, they all agreed that women were the ones more often penalized or rewarded.

An interviewee compared the different reactions about attractiveness of men and women in the workplace: "I love my boss and I respect him — I learn from him every day. But he's very, very overweight. If I were that overweight, I would not have my job. Women have the added burden of being attractive. Go into any corporation and sit in the cafeteria and look at the men and then look at the women. There are men who look like outright slobs. But a female slob won't make it. Even though we don't have to be Cindy Crawford, we still have to look good. There's some tolerance, but you still can't be severely overweight, and you've got to be chicly dressed."

One senior manager summed up her experience: "I know it's unjust, but I've noticed it year after year. For example, we bring in a hundred college students a year for internships. And there is — in my mind at least — a very, very big correlation between those students who are most attractive, vivacious, outgoing, and suave and those who receive offers and subsequent employment."

Flight attendant Cynthia Latham echoes that observation: "I see it all the time on the airplane. I work with some very beautiful women and some very handsome men, and I can see the reaction from the passengers. I see how their facial expressions change when there's a beautiful woman as opposed to an older man. They smile more; they're a little bit happier about the service."

Credibility is a by-product of both men's and women's appearance and grooming.

From another respondent: "I came out of a whole industry where looks are everything — television news. There are some intellectually mental midgets who are on the air because they have a look. I see it happen all the time. I can spend my whole life fighting that, or I can make an aggressive effort to look as good as I can. I have to say to myself, 'Get a grip, get over it, and do some things that will enhance your strengths.' Those are the options, because I don't think we're going to change that cultural mind-set in the foreseeable future."

An executive on the survey summed it up this way: "The difference is professional and unprofessional appearance. It's a way to establish quick credibility. People who don't package themselves well have to work harder for credibility."

Credibility is a by-product of both men's and women's appearance and grooming. A general counsel in a large oil company comments: "I see it in both my male and female lawyers, my direct reports. I have a woman in Houston who manages and grooms herself to a tee, and she is well received and liked by everyone. It's in part her grooming, in part her personality, and in part her skills. But it has been those first two attributes that have taken her to the top of this organization. Men don't necessarily like to have legal advice from a woman, particularly if a woman has to say, 'No, you can't do that, it's against the law.' I'll have another executive on our team appealing to me, 'We're going to make millions and millions, so don't let your lawyer stand in the way of this.' But I don't get that flak with this female lawyer, because her presence commands that kind of respect. You dress in a way that people look at you and say, 'Yes, you are successful, you probably know what you're speaking about. I'm going to listen to you.'"

Another senior manager agreed on the issue of credibility, saying that she sees nothing wrong with using appearance as one of her hiring criteria: "I have always felt that appearance tells a lot about a person — how they're organized and how they manage their life. My grandmother used to say that how a woman kept her house told a lot about her personality. I think that applies to personal appearance also."

Still another interviewee shared this experience: "I used to work with a woman at my last company who was thorough, organized, talented, and hard-working. By the time you got through giving her something to do, she had it done. But she was overweight and real short. People would discount her. I'd find myself saying to them, 'You just don't understand the talent this woman has, and if you'd give her a chance you'd find out that she's also really funny and charming.' But she didn't have any self-confidence because she knew she was overweight.

"Then something happened — I don't know what — and she began to lose weight. She gained more self-confidence. We practically worshipped her at this company. She was everything to us, the real backbone to the entire company, and the more we loved her, she just blossomed. It made me sad that it took people so long to get to know her for who she really was. I hate to feed into the problem our society has with the weight thing. It's terrible. I already see it with our kids; they're worrying about stuff like that already. But unfortunately, that's the way things are."

Several women went on to point out that it is also dangerous to be too good-looking. "I've had friends who are considered just absolutely beautiful, and they also have problems with self-esteem. They have trouble with being valued for things other than their looks. It's something they fight all the time." Others interviewees told tales of situations in which beautiful women were denied a job because somebody felt they "wouldn't fit in" and "wouldn't be taken seriously by our clients" or "wouldn't have credibility in the courtroom/classroom."

Some women are obsessed with their hair, their weight, their breasts, their thighs, their ankles, their freckles, and their wrinkles. But none of the smart women I interviewed mentioned being too concerned, even in jest, about any of these things. Their actual physical looks had become a non-issue, although their grooming, demeanor, and poise were still considered important.

Several women

went on to

point out that

it is also dangerous

to be

too good-looking.

All those surveyed elaborated on good looks to mean not just facial features or body structure and size. They also understood appearance to include grooming habits, appropriate clothes, and confident body language that reflected comfort and pleasure in one's appearance.

When I asked interviewees if they could tell me about women who may not be considered attractive, but who have developed a winning personality and attracted people to them, several stories tumbled out.

Here is one about a waitress in San Francisco's restaurant called Cliff House Park: "There is this waitress who has been in a little café overlooking the ocean for years. She's probably 5 feet tall and very substantially built. She's been there for about 40 years, but she always has a flower in her hair, wears fragrance, and remembers what you order. She's always happy and upbeat, whether she serves you fresh hot coffee, warm Danish, or fresh pie. She's enthusiastic about her food. If you were walking down the street past her, you wouldn't even look twice. But people go to that restaurant, including me, and wait in line to be seated at one of her booths."

That's a picture of someone who's comfortable with herself and has packaged herself well. Packaging also includes personality.

Another: "This woman in Tallahassee, a neighbor, was not attractive at all. But she always looked neat, with make-up and dress in style. She had this way of talking and listening to you. She gave you 100 percent attention. She would laugh and had a sense of humor that was just so appropriate. It was a flow, a thing that bubbled out of her. You just came away thinking, 'She's so great, so beautiful.' I don't have that gift, but I can sure spot it in others."

Another: "We have a female director here at the company [a large telecommunications firm]. She's probably in her late forties and has allowed her natural gray hair to come in. She's not a Raquel Welch type, but she has a friendly demeanor. She was raised in the south and she's very open and friendly. Accommodating. Remembers names. Remembers faces. She immediately puts people at ease at every level of the organization. Her friendliness, her receptivity, and her openness have earned her such a wonderful reputation here."

Packaging also includes personality.

Another: "Carolyn comes to mind. She's not a natural knockout beauty, but what makes her attractive is the interest she takes in other people. I've seen her stand in a crowded hallway with hundreds of women swarming around her and she'll be totally focused on one person, whoever she's talking to. That's her real key."

Another: "My boss. It's the simple things. Enthusiasm. She's always 'so happy you just came by' or just called. She may have a million other things going on at that minute, but you feel like you have her complete attention. She's a dynamo. Aggressive. Extremely smart. But no matter how much she's progressing herself, she brings a lot of other people along with her. She invests time in other people to help them achieve what they do best."

So what's the upshot here? Although appearance is still a major criteria for initial credibility, neither good looks nor deformity dictates destiny. Personality and skill matter most. We as a society don't care if your features and body (things you can't control) are beautiful; we do care about and draw conclusions about how you package and present yourself.

Regain Your Self-Respect Through Your Sense of Service and Satisfaction

If you still do not feel self-worth and value with the efforts already mentioned, consider your contribution to other people's lives. Are you building a serene home where your spouse and children can survive and thrive and accomplish their goals? Are you contributing to the community in some way through volunteer work at the school, the hospital, a hospice, a homeless shelter, or the voting poll?

Despite her total financial independence from successful ventures early in her career, one of the survey respondents points out that for some people, money has little to do with self-esteem. She explains: "I had a tremendous problem with self-esteem. I just didn't feel very valuable most of my life. What changed my life was starting to read the Bible and some management books. And then I remember running into the mother of one of my high school friends and she asked, 'How is it that you have changed so much?' I looked her right in the eye and answered, 'Because I have hurt so much.'"

Pain can be a great motivator — for those who ache and for those who serve them. Your own pain may be the pedestal from which you can lift other people out of the mire in their own lives. And if you choose to do that with your time, the joy and sense of satisfaction from helping to change other people's lives for the better can be an incredible source of your own self-respect.

Think about it: Mother Teresa, Florence Nightingale, and Eleanor Roosevelt have earned their place in history through other people's pain — and their service to those people.

Pain can be a great

motivator —

for those who ache

and for those who

serve them.

Regain Your Self-Respect Through Triumph Over Tragedy or Failure

Popular belief holds that confidence comes from your upbringing. Dr. Judith Briles, author of an excellent book on self-esteem and confidence, *The Confidence Factor,* argues that just the opposite is true. From her surveys of over 6,000 men and women summarized in the *Keri Report,* she discovered that confidence comes from crisis. The number-one professional "downer" was being fired or laid off from a job, and the most often cited personal tragedy was a breakup of a long-term relationship or marriage.

In other words, by bouncing back after a misfortune or a failure, people cut their teeth on the experience to gain confidence. Then more of those kinds of experiences stacked one on top of the other gradually build confidence that you can tackle the world.

...by bouncing back after a misfortune or a failure, people cut their teeth on the experience to gain confidence.

Jane Handly, now a beautiful fifty-year-old, became a success in large part from the strength she gained from overcoming adversity. As a four-year-old, Jane and her mother were coloring Easter eggs one day. When the doorbell rang and her mother left to answer it, Jane pulled her stool toward the stove and reached into the boiling pot of eggs. When she recoiled, the stool fell, and along with it the entire pot of scalding water. Jane was badly scarred neck to knees, permanent scars with her to this day.

The scars cover her shoulders, right breast, and trunk of her body. When she was a child, the scars started at her chin and crawled down both arms. She had to keep her hair cropped short because of the way the burns were located. She lost all teeth because of the scalding, and they didn't come back until she was eight. In her words, "I was a little toothless, scarred-up, short-haired, pitiful-looking child. The other children would say, 'Oh, good, Jane's here. We can play monster.'"

At age nine, Jane got bone cancer. She took megadoses of an early form of chemotherapy and lost a lot of her short-cropped hair. "I went to school from the first grade through the twelfth grade with the same kids. I was always 'Jane, the burned one.' And then when I was eighteen, my daddy entered me into the Miss Winston-Salem pageant. I was flabbergasted. Don't ask me why he did it or what he was thinking. I was totally in shock. I couldn't believe he'd done that. I kept saying, 'Daddy, I can't put on a bathing suit; I cannot do that.' And he said, 'Why not? If you look the judges right in the eyes, they won't see your scars.'"

Jane won the contest. When they crowned her, she began to experience the antithesis of her life to that point. As she tells it, that was the beginning of her triumph over tragedy. Many books, sermons, and therapists later, she insists that she has gained confidence and strength only because of, not in spite of, her tragedy.

Another respondent told about being a victim of an abusive spouse in an early marriage. When she discovered that her husband was being sexually unfaithful, she already had a young child and a very disabling physical impairment to deal with. She elaborates: "I overcame it by realizing that God allows — I don't want to say necessarily adversity — but opportunities in our life for us to choose to go one route or the other.

Smart women react to adversity with hope and confidence about the future.

"God never intended for me to hurt. He actually meant for me to have an abundant life. I actually came to see that I was a special person and that He loved me no matter what mistakes I might have made in my early life. He helped me to stay on track and never compromise my standard again as to what was right and wrong. I don't mean to imply [I had] a teenage pregnancy. Let's just say I was very young and very stubborn. I knew what was right and what was wrong and I chose to go the wrong way. Then God helped me to realize I was still a beautiful person — just the way I was."

Today, she is a successful, smart woman.

We've come full-circle. All those things that wounded your psyche and punctured your self-esteem long ago can be the very basis for future success. The bridge between the two "eras" is your reaction. Smart women react to adversity with hope and confidence about the future.

Learn to Learn, Learn to Earn

I know, I know — lifelong learning has become the newest management password. But it has been true a lot longer than it has been whispered in corporate halls.

Probably one of the most noted management consultants and professors of our era, Peter Drucker, still writes of his passion for learning. In a recent *Inc.* article, he tells about several learning experiences that taught him how to grow, to change, and to age without becoming a prisoner of the past.

In one particular learning situation, he tells about his stint on a newspaper as a journalist. He came in at six in the morning and finished by mid-afternoon, when the last edition went to press. So he began to force himself to study afternoons and evenings: international relations and international law, the history of social and legal institutions, and finance.

Learning never ends — if you're smart.

He writes, "Gradually, I developed a system. I still adhere to it. Every three or four years I pick a new subject. It may be Japanese art; it may be economics. Three years of study are by no means enough to master a subject, but they are enough to understand it. So for more than 60 years I have kept on studying one subject at a time. That not only has given me a substantial fund of knowledge. It has also forced me to be open to new disciplines and new approaches and new methods...."

Learning never ends — if you're smart. Here are some of the topics that surfaced in my interviews with smart women — skills, traits, and knowledge these women say they've learned *since the completion of their formal education:*

- communication
- people skills
- listening
- ability to give constructive feedback
- researching
- writing
- physics
- teamwork
- networking
- organizational skills

- teaching skills to other people
- hard work
- commitment
- reasoning and synthesizing information
- conflict resolution
- negotiation
- patience
- flexibility
- tolerance
- judgment and discernment
- computer skills
- real estate
- insurance
- accounting principles
- supervisory skills
- politics of how corporations work
- advertising and copywriting
- designing costumes, sets, and props
- playing handbells, oboe, banjo, clarinet, and guitar
- project management

The more degrees these smart women have — 86 percent have college degrees, 43 percent hold graduate degrees, and 12 percent, doctorates — the more skills, traits, and attitudes they seem to be able to identify that they didn't learn in the academic setting. Indeed, maybe some college professors or administrators reading this book will add a few courses to their curriculum!

Early on, smart women master the life skills important to every woman in today's world. By those essential life skills, I mean:

- interpersonal skills (listening, expressing your ideas, persuading, and resolving conflict),
- oral and written communication (organizing your ideas and information in writing and in front of a group clearly, concisely, and persuasively),
- time management (organization, planning, concentration, discipline, and dealing with procrastination),
- project management (planning, scheduling, budgeting,

● project management (planning, scheduling, budgeting, coordinating, delegating, executing, coaching, and evaluating), and

● financial savvy (prince charming may never appear, and if he does, he may know nothing about money management).

No matter how proficient in these areas — no matter how accomplished or how inexperienced — smart women continue to learn. They want to stretch their understanding so they can contribute to their own well-being and that of their family or business.

Joan Rivers, in her recent tour for her autobiography, *Bouncing Back,* talked about the terrible shock of having to learn finances and money management after her husband's suicide a few years ago. She insists that she didn't even know how to write a check. But she found out quickly on her road to learning how to support herself.

Smart women admit what they don't know and set about learning.

Smart women admit what they don't know and set about learning.

A recently published article in *Time* magazine cited several studies to point out the single most reliable indicator of a child's IQ was its mother's education. That's a sobering thought! Early in life, we learn that how others live their lives affects *us.* Only in later life do we learn that how we live our lives affects *others.* Our learning will impact our friends and family for decades.

Jane Handly sums up her enthusiasm for learning this way: "I read four or five books every week. I read across the board. Right now, I'm learning how you love your adult children differently than you love your ten-year-old. My teachers are everywhere. My church is a wonderful teacher for me. I go every week for two reasons: One, to stay prayed up, but the other reason is for the education I get there, unbelievably powerful education. I believe if you can pull out your stops, you control your life and you control your destiny. Like taking these acting classes, taking these dance classes, taking these exercises classes. Every morning I wake up and life's a school. I love that part of my life."

Smart women continue to learn. They learn from their failures. They learn from their successes. The question is not failure, per se. The question is, "Did you pick yourself up, dust yourself off, and move on down the road?" When you hit a bump in the road of life's journey, make it a habit to ask yourself, "What is the lesson here?" Lessons tend to keep arriving at our desk or doorstep until we master them.

There's no denying the harsh reality of the negative impact outside influences play on our psyches. Some women buckle under circumstances that make them uncomfortable or afraid. They suffer in silence rather than speak up with decisions that go against their best interests. They make no effort to improve bad situations. They quit. They suffer. They sulk.

But smart women take responsibility for themselves.

But smart women take responsibility for themselves. They learn, they grow, they change. Smart women *take responsibility for how others see them.* By their external composure and confidence, they clue the world in about what's inside.

Our society no longer births nobility. Everyone, from the president's rank on down, must build a reputation and create a perception of herself. You build the meaning your life holds. You build it by the skills you learn. You build it by the commitments you make and keep. You build it by the ethics you honor. You build it by the gifts you give.

In short, smart women create their own name badge.

In short, smart women create their own name badge.

Life is not a destination. Self-esteem is not a summit. Both continually unfold. Learning leads you to keep packing the resources you need to make the trip. You have money you have not yet earned. You have creativity you have not yet harnessed. You have energy you have not yet expended. You have intelligence you have not yet searched. You have talent you have not yet displayed. You have courage you have not yet tested. You have contributions you have not yet made.

3

Set Sail On Your Own Seas

We women have a difficult time knowing what success feels like. No, I don't mean we're not successful. It's just that we don't *feel* successful. We feel that somebody somewhere sometime slipped up, and we accidentally got labeled successful by mistake. Our conditioning has been to let others do the bragging — if there's any to be done.

Maybe we don't feel successful, because when someone uses that label about us, we're unsure about their definition. Smart women have learned to distinguish between worldly success and genuine success. They know there's a difference.

Worldly success involves earning academic degrees, holding high-paying jobs, winning industry awards, sending your children to prestigious universities, appearing on national television, autographing napkins, traveling around the globe and staying in five-star hotels, owning fine homes, and having a personal trainer and cook.

Genuine success involves feeling loved by your family, having friends that will come to your side in time of need, being excited to get out of bed every morning to get to your work, relishing a new thought until you've sucked every morsel from its truth, growing to your fullest potential as a person, feeling the satisfaction of making a difference in someone's life, improving the world for the next generation, feeling at peace with God.

There's nothing wrong with worldly success. I've been sailing toward that destination for a few years myself. But there's so much more to experience, so many more beautiful places to stop, so many more important places to dock.

Worldly success comes and goes, ebbs and flows. Genuine success seeps into your senses, all the way down to your bones.

Smart women define success in their own terms. They know which winds to catch. They like to sail toward both shores — worldly and genuine — but if pushed to choose one direction or the other, they'll seek genuine success.

Smart women define success in their own terms.

Find a Way to Make Your Passion Your Work

There is power in passion. Some people are afraid of it. Smart women are not. Smart women use passion to propel them toward their goals.

"Passion came long before I knew what it would look like," says Jane Handly. "Even as a little girl, I liked storytelling and writing down my thoughts. I came from a family of school teachers, so they encouraged that sort of thing. I was the first white woman in Winston-Salem to teach in an all-black school. There, I found out I could teach grammar through poetry, music, and art with those children. Then, at the age of 23, I was asked to make a movie for the Department of Public Instruction in North Carolina. It was called "For the Love of Learning," and was based on my experiences there.

Smart women use passion to propel them toward their goals.

"That unlocked the door that led me where I wanted to go. From that project I was given a full scholarship to get a master's degree in communication and theatre at Wake Forest. From that I was asked to speak at different places. It was like picking up a thread and following it. All along the way were these skills of speaking, writing, performing, sharing, and storytelling. The passion was there from the very beginning, but the specific goals unfolded. Once you've recognized your passion, you'll see the opportunities in front of you."

Society sometimes has a way of stifling our passion, even before we climb in the sailboat. As a child, we hear things like, "Just hold on." "Stop yelling." "Don't cry." "Stop that giggling." "Quit wiggling." "Don't squeal." Sit down." "Wait your turn." "Don't get so excited."

Then as an adult wanting to sail along with the wind in our hair, we hear admonitions like: "Slow down, take your time." "Just cool your heels." "Rome wasn't built in a day." "Put it in idle, will you?" "Just back off a bit." "Don't get so worked up about this." "If it ain't broke, don't fix it." "Why not just let things cool down a little?" "Just don't rock the boat." "Let's not make waves." "You've got to get everybody aboard." "Let's not go off on a tangent here."

We're lucky if we make it to our first job without someone trying to "tone us down." But those who survive with their passion intact find it like nourishment to the soul. When you meet people with passion, it shows — on their face, in their eyes, and in their movement. Passion is even in the Bible, which tells us that whatever our hand finds to do, we should do it with all our might.

"Do what you love and the money will follow." But is it true? If you really do what you love, will you still have money to pay the mortgage? Yes. Will you still have money to buy the luxuries? Yes and no. That depends on how you define the luxuries — as jewelry or happiness.

Granted, this whole idea takes a lot of courage — even to think about the possibilities. But then smart women have courage. They dare to dream.

To follow your passion, consider: What would you do every day if your time was your own? I know, I know — sleep. But after you got rested? What would you do if you didn't have to worry about buying groceries?

One interviewee laughs about a conversation she once had with a friend who had left her law practice. The friend called one day to give her an update on the new job: "You were right; I made a huge mistake in leaving my old job."

"How did you decide that?"

"I was looking at my watch."

"What are you talking about?"

"I was looking at my watch. I've never in the entire time I practiced law looked at my watch without saying, 'Oh, my goodness, it's already six o'clock,' or 'It's already too late.' Today, I just looked at my watch and thought, 'It's three o'clock; when's it ever gonna be five?'"

Our awareness of time — passing or standing still — reveals great truths! What would engage you so deeply that you'd forget to look at the clock? What would you do even if no one wanted to pay you to do it?

What would engage you so deeply that you'd forget to look at the clock?

For me, that's writing. At the age of 28, I had begun my second year of teaching Spanish at a middle school. The first year was exciting; the second year was not. With all the teaching plans done and the extra enrichment activities inserted, I felt the wind go out of my sails. I needed a new challenge. Here was the conversation that followed in a friend's office:

He said, "So what else would you like to do?"

"I don't know what else there *is* to do." We lived in a rather small town at the time.

"No," he corrected me. "I didn't ask you, 'What else *is there* to do?' I asked you, 'What would you *like* to do?'"

"Well, I have an English degree. But I don't know what else I can do with an English degree but teach."

"No," he corrected me again. "I'm not talking jobs. I'm talking about, 'What do you *like* to do?' What's fun to you? What do you enjoy?"

There was a long pause, during which my entire short life passed in front of my eyes. "Write. English compositions. That used to be fun for me. Other kids hated it, but I just *loved* it. I'd work on a composition all weekend — just for the fun of it." I looked at him intently. "But how can somebody make a living writing?"

What would you do even if no one wanted to pay you to do it?

"I don't know. I've never known anybody who was a writer. But I'd suggest you find out."

So I did. I drove to the public library and checked out every book they had on the topic of writing, from *How To Write the Great American Novel* to *Writing Jokes and Newspaper Fillers*. I drove home and read almost around the clock for four weeks. I taught myself the industry and the techniques to get started. With the typewriter sitting in the corner of the bedroom on a folding table, I was in business.

From the very beginning, it was passion that pushed me. I remember waking at 5:00 a.m., or earlier on many mornings, forcing myself to stay in bed until my husband's alarm went off so I wouldn't wake him, then puttering to the keyboard. I bounced my daughter on my shoulder with one arm while pecking at the keys with one hand to finish a paragraph. I took my research books to the baseball field to read between the innings and until my son got up to bat. After I put the kids to bed in the evenings, I wrote well past midnight because I "just wanted to make one more point." I've missed parties that I intended to make because I simply forgot to look at the clock on a Friday or Saturday night. I've sat behind the computer for twelve hours without realizing I'd not eaten all day.

Passion. That's what we're talking about here. Passion about finding genuine satisfaction from the work you do. Although senior executive Rebecca Noecker stresses that her priority for the past 23 years has been her husband and her two boys, the passion for her work still burns: "I've found something that I just *really like*. I'm happy to come to work every day. I'm happy to work long hours, because what I'm doing is a challenge. I just *thrive* on it." You can hear it in her voice.

When questioned about whether they felt passionate about their work, only one in five of those surveyed responded that they did *not*. Those 20 percent spoke about their lack of passion with a sigh:

- "I used to be passionate about it. But not anymore."
- "No, I'm not doing what I want to be doing. Right now, I'm in a position where it's a struggle to produce outcomes that I think are valuable."
- "I've thought a lot about it. The problem is that I feel like I've devoted so much time to this career, it would be hard to switch. My passions are all avocation activities, such as genealogy and decorating. That's the problem with career success. When you're very good at something, it's very hard to quit. I secretly wish, when our company was going through all the layoffs, that something bad would have happened to

force me to change careers. It's when things are going so well, you're afraid to rock the boat."

● "I'd rather be doing something else, like something that I felt was going to matter, to be frank. I have a lot of business background and would just hate to throw that away. But for example, I'd like to be managing a business office for a homeless outreach service, or doing something where I could see clearly at the end of it that I'm doing something that helps someone."

● "I've been eighteen years with this one organization, and I'm very entrenched in the compensation and benefit structure. So my passion is not important enough for me to exit the corporate world."

● "I have always used my career only as a way to survive. If I had had my choice, I probably would have gone into acting or modeling or something. I wanted to be more glamorous, but Mom told me to do something that would always support me. So it was going to be nursing. I did that, and sat around and waited for prince charming. I saw my life as just temporary until my *real life* started. And that didn't happen until age 33, when I got married. At some point in those years, actually around age 30, I figured out that I probably wasn't going to meet prince charming and that I'd better find a better way to take care of myself. I started thinking nursing salaries would max out soon, and if I were looking at providing for my own retirement, I needed to do better. I come from a family of lawyers, so I went to night law school and got that second degree. It was a survival thing. It just evolved."

As a footnote, this last comment comes from a smart woman who has now opted for full-time, stay-at-home motherhood, a choice she does finally feel passionate about.

But the overwhelming majority (80 percent) of those interviewed spoke passionately about what they do and the satisfaction they derive from it.

Get the Vision

Fulfillment comes from pursuing a passion. Passion

pushes us to a vision. Finally, a vision leads to goals.

Dru Scott Decker, Ph.D. and author of *Stress That Motivates,* has one of the more explicit visions that houses her lifetime goals: "I've had certain things that I want to accomplish — my lifetime goals. The system I've used is to picture myself at my 100th birthday party. I've had the picture since I was about 30. I'd come into the party and have on this burgundy silk, mid-calf skirt and a leotard. I come in and do this very agile little dance. I'm hosting a beautiful dinner, with candles and crystal and beautiful linens. Now when you think about this dinner and this dance, that means keeping my body in shape, stretching, eating the right things, and earning some money to pay for the dinner for all my friends.

"The other picture is of a woman on the beach in Hawaii. I grew up in a very humble situation, with not many resources, and I had this picture that when you get old, you're not going to have any money. But one day in Hawaii, I was walking down to meet a client about 6:45 in the morning, and I saw this woman walking back up the street from the beach to her apartment in Honolulu, after an early-morning swim. She had gray hair pulled up in this little knot, and her towel was tossed across her shoulder. I started picturing that as another part of my 100th birthday party. That vision captures most of my lifetime goals."

The overriding thing about passion is that you can't compartmentalize it.

When you feel passionate about how you are spending your time, you can't decide whether to call it work or play. The passion and vision may be about your personal goals or career goals. The overriding thing about passion is that you can't compartmentalize it. The passionate feeling spills over into your consciousness twenty-four hours a day.

Jeanne O'Connor-Green, senior project manager at Amoco, agrees about having a passion at work: "The first step in any goal-setting is to have a goal *vision.* Then once I start to get my arms around what that vision means, I get more concrete about the steps that will be required in order to accomplish that vision. In fact, I go through that exercise with my customers. My mission, basically, is to help improve the organization through improved performance of people."

Dr. Sallie Hightower says, "My passion, my absolute passion, is to engage in new, creative, challenging work — really breakthrough, cutting-edge stuff. The more never-been-done-before kind of things, the better."

Whether they call it a vision or a goal, respondents emphasize the importance of big-picture thinking. Kathy Harless, president of a subsidiary of a large tele-communications company, says, "I think we women have a tendency to stay too focused on the details and forget the overall picture. I think that's because we are very multi-task. We can bounce lots of balls in the air, and we really need to make sure we've got the overall big-picture, the vision."

Amy Quigley Rudy considers her entire entrepreneurial business as a goal on the way to living the bigger vision: "To grow my business is one of my goals, but it's a vehicle to get to the point where I am serene. Right now it's pretty frantic, juggling and massaging and finessing and trade-showing and all you've got to do as part of that. But my goal really is to raise a family, to spend quality time with them, and to have the means to do what we want to do."

Stephanie Zweben, manager of Human Resources in a Fortune 500 company, says, "I set my goal to be well-educated. So I have two new master's degrees, a teacher certification, and all kinds of certifications in other areas."

The vision may have to be broad at first, and then get narrower at the point of embarkation. But passion pushes us toward a vision and enables us to accomplish the goals to bring the vision into reality.

Those who live by goals know that goals need to be specific to be real motivators.

Be Specific About Your Goals

Those who live by goals know that goals need to be specific to be real motivators. Most people outline these steps in their goal-setting: Be specific. State your goals positively. Add a deadline. Develop an action plan. Chart your progress.

Amy Quigley Rudy has set herself a rugged climb with the specificity of her business goals: "I want to grow ModelOffice into a $50 million company by the year 2000. And at that point, I want to go public. Other things are the stepping-stones to get to that main goal."

"My goal was to get a patent," says Jennifer Raymond, technical manager at Frito-Lay. "I did that. Just today, it landed on my desk. It's for developing a new process for making potato chips. I don't know how much external fanfare it will get, but I feel terribly proud of it."

Financial planning expert Judith Briles, Ph.D., says, "One of our *material* goals this year is that we're going to actually build our dream home. We're in the process of doing that now. That's why I'm sitting down tomorrow to do goal setting. We're going to put it together in a treasure-map format so we can visualize it and see it with words and pictures every day."

Carolyn Corbin, Ph.D. and founder of several small businesses, has made it a lifelong habit to set goals: "In high school, I set my goal to be valedictorian, and I was. Then when I went to college, I set my goal to graduate summa cum laude. I did that. Then for eight years I was in the computer industry in aerospace doing computer instruction. That was my goal because there were so few women in aerospace. Then I went from there to banking, and I set my goal to be the youngest woman elected officer of a major US bank. I did that. From there, I started selling insurance; within four months, I made the Million Dollar Roundtable. Then when I decided to go into speaking, I set my goal to win the international competition in Toastmasters. I won the title in the US and in Mexico. That gave me confidence that I could make it in the speaking business."

Goals push us.

Goals pull us.

Goals define us....

Goals push us. Goals pull us. Goals define us.

Add Deadlines

One respondent observes a "before" and "after" difference — before and after deadlines: "About two years ago, I made a list of things that I wanted to do, and put some very aggressive dates on them — everything from making x amount of dollars in my business to very specific things like getting product into distribution, meeting the right person, and getting married. None of them happened when I thought they would. But at least it gave me a timeline or milestone to shoot for. The deadlines have definitely made a difference."

She has identified the key issue about deadlines: Putting deadlines on goals is not about making things happen when we think they should. Having a deadline does not mean that we don't relinquish control and change course when change is in order. The difference a deadline makes is in attitude. When we're afraid to add deadlines, generally it's because we've not yet made the commitment to the goal and we're not sure we're ready to expend the energy required to get there.

And that's okay! Deadlines or no deadlines is not the point; our willingness or hesitancy to commit to them is. Let's just say that setting a deadline is taking your pulse rate to measure the passion behind the goal.

Develop an Action Plan

Smart women survey their resources. They do a mental or even a literal checklist: Who do I need to know? How much money do I need? What experiences should I have? What information do I need to master?

Smart women survey their resources.

Dr. Eloise Fields considers education a major bag from which you draw resources to succeed for a lifetime. Talking from experience with her three degrees, she says, "Don't worry about not having money to get an education. Just go to school. You can get the money somewhere. I don't believe in waiting. You can work your life around education. It's that important."

Jane Brimmer, senior manager at US West says, "I plan to get an international business assignment. I've had some sponsorship from one of our officers here, and I went to the Harvard Advanced Management Program."

Jeanne O'Connor-Green outlines her process for bringing about performance improvement in a particular department at Amoco: "I help them [customers] 'frame in' what a change means and what it's going to take in order for that change to happen. I want them to be really specific about the steps they must go through. It works in business with internal clients and it works in my personal life."

Carolyn Corbin had an ambitious action plan from the very beginning: "In order to be able to go into the speaking business, I went into the life insurance business. I could work during the day building a speaking business, and I could make money working at night selling insurance. I became an insurance broker as a means to an end. Within four years, I quit doing insurance and went totally into the speaking business." Her plan got her there.

Executive Kathy Harless says: "I knew early on that in order to progress in the corporation there were certain jobs I would have to take. I knew every one of those jobs meant moving out of Texas to headquarters. I always described that to myself as going to get my corporate lunch ticket punched. Man or woman, it didn't matter. I had to have those experiences. They widened and broadened my thought processes."

These smart women haven't zig-zagged here and there without a purpose and a plan.

These smart women haven't zig-zagged here and there without a purpose and a plan.

Chart Your Progress Along the Way

How close are you to the goal? Are you losing or gaining ground? In the beginning of my writing career, charting progress on my activities proved to be the only way I could tell whether I was moving or sitting still. All the books on writing careers told me that I if wanted to get published in major magazines I needed to send query letters to editors suggesting possible article topics and asking for assignments. These advisors assured me that my first efforts would be met with rejection, but that I must keep circulating those query letters and articles nonetheless.

So how else would I know if I were making progress while no checks were coming in the door? Keep a chart of activity. I literally made a list of each article or query letter as I developed it, and then charted its path through the mail from one magazine editor to the next. Each rejection letter that returned to me meant that I must be one notch closer to publication.

Now, almost twenty years later, the principle holds true

for managing sales reps in my communication training company. Before I recruited and hired the first salespeople, I naively asked a far more experienced manager: "The sales cycle takes so long in our business — how do you know if that new rep is getting anywhere the first few months that you're paying his or her salary and don't see sales coming in the door?"

Answer: "Chart their progress. Manage their activity. Make sure they take the tiny learning and planning steps along the way until they start to make the sales."

When you see there's no progress on your own chart of activities, begin asking some questions of yourself: Do you have *reasons* or *excuses* for not meeting your goals? How do you *feel* about not meeting the goal?

If you feel regret at not meeting your goal, what course corrections are in order? If there is no regret, then maybe you should toss out the goal and live happily ever after doing something else.

A goal should feel like a guide, not a gun to your head!

A goal should feel like a guide, not a gun to your head!

Reevaluate Your Commitment to Your Vision or Goals; Modify Them or Toss Them Out

Carolyn Corbin reevaluated about eight years ago and did a course correction: "My passion changed. That's basically what happened. All my life, I wanted to be a speaker. I used to go in the 70's to the rallies and listen to Zig Ziglar and Norman Vincent Peale, all the time thinking, 'I want to do that. I want to do that more than I want to eat. I'm willing to do whatever it takes to be on the speaking circuit, to be the best.' I wanted it so badly that I could taste it, chew it, and spit it out. I was just driven. Then I wrote the book *Strategies 2,000*. I had been speaking before that, but that book's release was the turning point. That put me on the road all over the world.

"I got to do what I wanted to do, and then all at once.... Did I burn out? Did I start setting new priorities? I don't know. But something changed right in the middle of all that. I thought, 'If I'm getting what I want, why am I so dissatisfied?' I realized that to follow that passion of speaking I had to travel all the time, and to travel all the time took me away from home and my friends and my husband. I missed home and all the relationships I cherished. That wasn't what I wanted at all. So I changed course."

Angie Casey also did a course correction mid-sea: "A couple of years ago I had to decide whether to stay in management or go back to a more technically oriented systems analyst position. I really felt like people would think that was a step backward in my career. There are just things I like to do better than project management — that's too much stress and too much mundane work. The company considers them [technical and managerial positions] parallel paths, but there is still this aura around having a manager title. To give up that career path to switch into something that is maybe less glamorous-sounding, but something that I enjoy doing, didn't make a lot of sense financially. But my husband and I talked about it, and he wanted me to do what made me happiest. So that's what I did. I get to work with customers and actually have the satisfaction of solving real problems."

It takes courage to change course. But then, smart women have courage.

Eloise Fields also understands that goals can enable or enslave. "Vision is more important than goals. Goals emerge and change as necessary when we have the big-picture vision in the mind."

Dora Grider, president of her own mortgage company, adds, "I don't write goals because I get tunnel vision. Things change." Laurie Barringer agrees: "I don't want to get so locked into my daytimer or my goals that I miss God moving me in another way. I can get very structured and focused down a tunnel, and if He wants me to do something else, I can miss it completely. I've got to check my thinking all the time."

It takes courage to change course. But then, smart women have courage.

Know What Makes You Run Aground

The surest way to get hung on dead-center is taking our eyes off *our* destination. That's not to say we don't adapt our travel to others in our lives, but trying to live our lives through other people presents major problems.

Part owner and manager of a medium-sized insurance agency, Lynelle Goff Eddins knows the fallout of trying to borrow someone else's goals: "I don't know if you'd say that I was living goals through another person, but obviously in my first marriage I really didn't have very many goals. I pretty much lived my life trying to help my husband accomplish *his* goals. Although there's not a lot of contentment or reward in that, it cuts short your own ability to grow and learn. You have to feel some accomplishment on your own. That was the source of a great deal of my lack of confidence about my own abilities for awhile."

Mothers sometimes have difficulty in encouraging their children to explore their interest while not imposing on them their own passions and visions. A young mother confides: "Sometimes with the girls I find myself trying to make them perfect in some way. I have to really watch myself to make sure I'm not pushing them into things that they don't want to do. Like with my daughter's piano. Sometimes I have to sit down and ask her, 'Do you like this? Am I just trying to make you do this for me?'"

The difference between a push and a shove is more than the force; it's the passion with which it's done.

But smart women correct their course.

On surveys about contentment or dissatisfaction among single and married men and single and married women, the "married woman" segment of our population continually reports the highest dissatisfaction with life. Why? Can it be that many women arrive at midlife feeling adrift, unfulfilled, and bored? Their grown children have left home to follow their own dreams. Their spouse stands at the height of a rewarding and successful career. Their friends seem engaged in varied activities giving meaning to their lives. These women may have been sailing on someone else's sea too long, with no thought for where they are headed and where they will end up when the boat docks.

It happens. But smart women correct their course.

Smart women define success in their own terms: Success

may mean holding an executive position in a Fortune 500 company. Success may mean learning new skills. Success may mean raising well-adjusted kids. Success may mean running a mission in Mozambique. Success may mean providing excellent customer service. Success may mean winning the starring role in a Broadway play. Success may mean growing your own company.

Smart women set sail on their own sea of success. They find and stir the passion inside them until it becomes the flame that sweeps them into *genuine* success — personal fulfillment.

4
Put Up or Shut Up

Smart women decide things — and then move on.

For whatever reason, other women whine, complain, and blame. They feel helpless, hurt, angry, or confused over situations and relationships. Women often make excuses for what's not happening — not necessarily excuses for themselves, but excuses for other people and why they behave like they do.

From a friend considering a second marriage: "No, he's not working now, but he'll find something. He just has a problem with his temper; he always gets angry at his bosses and quits without thinking things through. He's not very close to the kids, but that's because they're so spoiled and he refuses to spoil them. Yes, sometimes he says hurtful things to me, but he doesn't really mean them. He's really trying to get his life together, and when we get married, he's going to...."

What's wrong with this picture? A woman is about to make a decision based on emotion (love, hope, or fear?) rather than logic.

From a friend unhappy in her job: "I feel like my talents are really wasted in my job. I've gone to training classes and gotten the job experience I need to move up, but when I mention anything about a transfer to my manager, she gets irate and yells at me. She says I'm just trying to mess up her department, that I don't have the skills or judgment to get a better job. But I think she says that just because she doesn't

Smart women decide things — and then move on.

want to have to train somebody else. Underneath her bark, she really appreciates me. So I guess I'll just stay put until she agrees to help me get the transfer."

What's wrong with this picture? A woman is about to make a decision based on emotion (hope, timidity?) rather than logic.

From a friend involved in an entrepreneurial venture: "When Susan and I started this business together, we both agreed on our roles. But this last year, she lost interest, and she's not pulling her weight. So I'm having to do her job and mine. I'm beginning to resent her. I'd say something about it to her, but I don't want to destroy our friendship."

What's wrong with this picture? A woman is struggling with a decision based on both logic and emotion.

The biggest energy waster — the biggest stresser — the biggest career mistake for women — is indecision. Not to decide is to decide. Smart women decide things by design, not default.

Smart women decide things by design, not default.

Why Do We Dally Around with Decisions?

We fear making the wrong decisions, but all decisions are not created equal. All decisions are not irreversible. We have to learn to distinguish the important from the trivial, and make or delegate the trivial decisions immediately so we have time for the important decisions.

A second reason: We fear taking responsibility for ourselves. Our whole society has become so focused on women as victims that we fail to see our choices and options. We're victims of verbal abuse. We're victims of physical abuse. We're victims of sexual abuse. We're victims of alcoholic parents. We're victims of dysfunctional families. We're victims of spoiled teens. We're victims of discrimination in hiring. We're victims of fraudulent merchants. We're victims of divorce court. The list goes on.

All of these things are real, no doubt, but the point is that victims remain helpless. Only when we decide to act do we gain power over our lives. We have to let go of past injustices and act *in spite of them.*

One respondent who's happily married now and describes it as "heaven on earth" shares this about her first marriage: "We were married for 19 years and all of the 19 years were deadly, horrible, and awful. I would describe them as fearful, abusive, insecure, mean, unfulfilling, and dishonest. He had always threatened to kill me so I knew that was a real possibility. I was so afraid of him that I made my child timid. Even to this day, at 29 years old, he can't tell you how he feels or what he wants. He's having to go to therapy to work through that, because I was so afraid he'd make his daddy angry. We didn't have honest feelings or thoughts in our house. It was a facade, and it was a festering sore for 19 years. Wasn't that a lovely thing? I stayed because what would *they* say if I left? Well, *they* wouldn't say anything; *they* don't care. Whoever *they* are."

The smart women have decided not to remain victims. They do something. They decide and they take action.

Learn To Make the Hard Decisions

It didn't take me long in consulting with senior executives in client organizations to substantiate the published research that there is a basic difference in how the genders make decisions. In a nutshell, it's this: Men value fast decisions; women value thorough decisions.

That natural inclination to take our time, to weigh, to analyze, and to gather input can be aggravated most especially when the decision looming large before us involves tough choices with dire consequences.

We as a gender don't take our decision making lightly. Very, very few of the women surveyed considered themselves emotional decision makers. Most described their process laboriously, many using Ben Franklin's pros-and-cons chart.

Debra Hertzog, currently a stay-at-home mom and community leader, even used that method to marry her mate of 17 years: "Most all of my decisions are very calculated; they are over analyzed. I put on paper the pros and cons. I don't make many decisions emotionally. The decision to marry was well thought out. Because I always wanted to

The smart women have decided not to remain victims.

marry and share my life with somebody at some point, it was low on the priority list until after I'd done other things. It was something I wanted when the time and the place and the person arrived. This all happened overseas in Germany when I was into my teaching career and had accomplished several personal goals — graduate school, traveling, living overseas, and being independent from my dad before I became someone's wife. Then I met the person and developed the relationship. The calculation was about being ready for the commitment, having found the person who had the qualities I admired."

Sound decision making.

Other hard decisions face us on the job. Myra Puryear, customer relations manager for a large auto-leasing organization, says that some of the most difficult decisions she faces are those involving a customer request. "We had a customer who had recently been diagnosed with a terminal illness. Basically, she wanted us to forego the entire debt on her car. She sent us her medical background and a chronicle of her story. It was her way of validating her story. We did look at opportunities to minimize the impact, but we were not able to absorb that obligation on her behalf. It's hard to say, 'I want to do this, but I can't.'"

Lynelle Goff Eddins, part owner and manager of an insurance agency, talks about big dollars riding on her decisions. "I just dealt with negotiating our way out of a lease last year. We were right on the issues, and emotionally I wanted to go to court and fight the trustee all the way to the courthouse if I had to. But I knew that that was an emotional reaction, not a business decision. So we decided to buy our way out of the lease at a reasonable rate. It was definitely the right decision, because we would have spent three times that much to take it to court."

Vice President of Product Development Katy Crane recalls a difficult decision with terminating a long-time employee she considered a friend. "He was with me from the beginning, my first hire. He and I were in the office, digging the trenches together, but he just couldn't do the job anymore. For months we worked with him to get his territory sales numbers up. He did try, but he just wasn't able to do it. He wasn't happy here either, being at the bottom of the pile. So we had to terminate him. I just had to come to the conclusion that he needed to move on, and I needed to help him move on."

Martha Castillo, a senior executive with Praxair, has this to share about her calculating methodology in a job decision: "After law school, I was recruited by GE and went to work with them. GE is such a big, well-respected company, but ultimately I left them. I have to say it was the most difficult decision of my life, because there was really no good reason to leave. Then I analyzed this other company. It seems so silly to say, but you put together a list of all the things you want to compute: the people, the responsibilities, and the size of the office. I'm very methodical in my decision making. I put it all on paper. I could actually weigh it. I got a number. The interesting thing was about three to four years after taking the job, I rediscovered this worksheet. I had done pretty well in terms of my expectations — from how I rated the cafeteria to the responsibilities I would be given. That's very refreshing and defining at times."

"I'm very methodical in my decision making."

Jeanine Brannon, now running her own company, at one time worked for a large utility company. She talks about repositioning herself in the company with a well-thought-out action plan: "I had aspirations to move out of administrative areas, but there were very few women in any kind of responsible positions at that time. The year I finished my degree, I decided that I had to reposition myself, so I sat down with my plan. I realized that I had to go to the president of the company to share my plan with him and see if I could get support at the top. If I could get support, I felt I had a future there. If I couldn't get support, I knew that it would do no good with the middle people.

"It took me weeks to get up the courage. I built a formal plan for it, and I kept that formal plan with me daily so I could change it. I built a dialog so I would be comfortable with what I was going to say, and I had people role play it with me —

what he might say. I did meet with him eventually and he was semi-receptive, enough that I felt like I could build a future there. Within a period of a few months, I was offered some good opportunities. I stayed there fifteen years."

Such methodical decision making was true with smart women making personal or professional decisions. Mistakes in personal situations can be just as disastrous, if not more so, from love relationships to schools for your children. But the vast majority of the smart women interviewed describe this same methodical decision making as the method that pays off most often in the most satisfactory way.

One of my toughest decisions combined both the business and the personal, for a double-whammy if things hadn't turned out as I had hoped. Being unsure how much longer my first husband could hold a job, I began to understand that I would eventually become the sole support for my two children. At that point, I had decided to form a communications training company. For the next ten years, I operated the company out of Houston, first from a home office and then from larger offices outside. It was during this ten years that my first marriage finally collapsed. I had to get serious about making a living for the family and sending my kids to college. At that point, I also decided that I wanted to move myself and the kids back to the Dallas area to be closer to my parents and brother and sister and their families.

Here was my dilemma: Research said that a consulting firm that moved its location from one city to another typically lost one-third of its clients. I couldn't afford to cut my billings by a third. Yet, the emotional pull was strong. I wanted to live close to my family, to be home for all the holidays, to talk on the phone every day, to drop by their houses on a whim for no reason at all.

I toyed with the idea for a year: to move and risk losing business or not to move and feel lonely, separated from the emotional support of my family. I reasoned, the older my parents got, the more urgent I would feel the need to be near them. By the end of a year of vacillating between the two choices, another major factor entered the decision picture. I

Such methodical decision making was true with smart women making personal or professional decisions.

had met someone special. Before long, we decided to marry.

My new husband joined me in the business, and he was willing to make the leap to Dallas if I was. We settled on our plan of breaking the news to clients who had come to expect me to be in their office within an hour of their call. Methodically, I met with client after client over lunch to tell them that I was moving the company to be nearer family. I assured them of my commitment to the continued personal service from us despite the new location, and ended with, "I hope this doesn't cost me your business."

I moved. They stayed. Through the transition, we retained every single client. It was not until a couple of years after the move to Dallas that I realized the enormity of the consequences had clients not given me their loyalty. It was a tough decision, with both business and personal consequences hanging in the balance. I didn't like decision dilemmas then; I don't like decision dilemmas now. But I haven't figured a way around them, in either business or personal life.

Jeanne O'Connor-Green tells about her weighed decision on house buying — where many of us lean to heart: "We made a chart of all the things we needed to have in a house and then prioritized things. Then we put a ranking on each item. I measured each house that way, and I ended up buying a house that was perfect. It fit every criteria that we said we had to have and most of the ones we said we wanted. It really did help to overcome an emotional decision to buy the house just because we loved the color of the walls."

Jane Handly applied the "listing analysis" to her choice of husband: "The smallest risk I ever took was marrying Bob. He was like a miracle. He was my prayer answered. I had made a list of 32 things I wanted in a husband, and he had 30 of them. Unbelievable. And he literally showed up at my door. I mean, literally. I had seen him on television and didn't even know his name or that he lived here. He literally knocked on my door, and there stood the man. It has been magical ever since."

For her, logic and love collided for a perfect impact. Jane had done her thinking, put together her list, and had been duly diligent before commitment. When Bob appeared, romance was ripe. Sure, it's romantic to think about being swept off your feet, so in love that a "decision" to marry becomes a moot issue, but the divorce courts stay full of those kinds of relationships. Whether in love, in debt, or in death, decision making requires more substantive thinking.

In case you are currently facing a tough decision that has you stalled, here are the key steps in good decision making:

- State clearly the issue, situation, or problem.
- Identify the criteria as a basis for the decision.
- Develop options.
- Measure the options against the criteria.
- Decide and act.

Good decisions, both at work and at home, lead to satisfying relationships and sound business situations.

Take Calculated Risks

Some decisions require risk.

Some decisions require risk. The large majority of women who have taken big risks look back with several emotions: amazement, relief, exhilaration, gratitude, and peace.

Deborah Tyler, a single woman who started her own business several years ago, sums up the common risk-taking reflection like this: "There were so many unknowns. The resources weren't there. The finances weren't there. The networking really wasn't in place. But I was passionate about it and convinced that it was an idea whose time had come. I would say it definitely has paid off, that is, in terms of what it has done for me. Even in evaluating the risks — and I knew the enormous risks going in — one of my deciding points came sitting in a hotel room. I thought, 'I'd rather take a risk, fail, and pay for this endeavor for the rest of my life than not to take the risk and end up at age 92 sitting on the front porch wondering what would have happened if....'"

Decisions mean risk — some little, some big — so we plan with the end in mind. An engineer friend advised me twenty years ago when I was just on the verge of setting up my business: "Never set up any kind of business deal or partnership that you don't know how to get out of. Things can go sour quickly." I learned to plan from a worst-case scenario, rather than an eyes-closed optimism.

At one point, I made the decision to hire a chief operating officer at a big six-figure income. Looking back, I did not check references as diligently as I should have and took too much information on face value without supporting evidence. But at least I had done some of my homework. I knew how much money I was willing to risk and how long I could give him to prove his worth. At the end of a year when he had not met our agreed-upon goals, I had to let him go. Although his salary was a big "ouch" on the bottom line, we did plug the hole. I had considered the end before we began.

That is not to say the future belongs to the pessimists. It does not! Those who shape the future must believe in it. Some in the last three decades have found it fashionable to be cynical. You have probably read this saying on one of those office plaques somewhere: "Pessimists got that way by financing optimists."

But smart women who plan to make a difference in the world have to believe that a difference can be made.

But smart women who plan to make a difference in the world have to believe that a difference can be made.

An attorney thinks back on her decision to stay at home with her new baby: "We had two incomes, then I found out I was going to have a baby. I really wanted the security of the second income. My husband's job could fluctuate some, being in the health-care industry, and it could be very, very scary. The decision to take time off and be home with the baby really released the safety net under me — that second income — but, it has paid off. Somehow God has blessed our finances, and they have stretched to more than I could have imagined. I'm happier that I'm getting to invest this time with Allison."

Eloise Fields was working as a dean at a university when they needed an extra $100,000 for a particular program. "That amount was totally out of reason for any one college. But after prayer about the issue, I became clear that I needed to forge ahead. I put groups of us deans together to talk to the Chancellor, and we got our $100,000. Of course, the state legislature had to approve it after the chancellor submitted it to the state, but in effect, it was that approach — the organized meetings and groups that I stuck my neck out to put together — that did it. Reason said it couldn't be done, but we did it."

Some risks force us to put dollars on the line that we don't yet have. Amy Quigley Rudy explains one such risk: "I recently signed the best webfarm in the country for software distribution, and it's very expensive. We had to go with forgivable draws with them, which is a sort of retainer. Logically, I knew that we couldn't afford them. But at this point, I knew in my heart that bringing them on was going to open some doors that had been closed. Logically, we couldn't do it, but I signed the contract. The first couple of months were tough, but they [the webfarm] stuck it out with us. All of their people are really hungry, proactive, and responsive. They've done their best work with us, and now all the sales are closing. I was willing to roll the dice with them, and it's paying off. It was definitely the right move."

Dora Grider, owner of a mortgage company, remembers what it was like to put her entire future in hock: "When I started my business here as a mortgage broker, I had worked for Shearson-Lehman and for Chase for eight years. They gave me a great background, and I left a good income. Then, when I left to open this business, I committed to a five-year lease. My husband and I personally signed for it. To me, that was a huge risk. We had enough to equip the office as far as investment, but everything else was going to come from my production of loans. My income was going to be zero until I started to close loans. We had two kids in college at the time, and about that time my husband decided he wanted to change careers and become a pilot! We laughingly now call it our midlife crisis."

Another senior executive, Ann-Marie Stephens, talks about going back for her MBA later in life and leaving a well-paying job at a very stable company for a new venture: "I viewed it as a big risk. My experience at Proctor and Gamble was great; I knew that I could always fall back on that. But the biggest risk I took was the loss of income [in going back for my

MBA]. You're a much older student in a job market that is really targeted to younger adults. So a lot of the people coming in to interview have less experience than what you bring to the table as the candidate. The valuing of your experience versus their point of reference was very difficult. In that regard, it was risky.

"Then the people around you sometimes doubt the wisdom of going back. They say things like, 'What can they teach you? — there's nothing there.' You're risking the chance that they may be right, that you'll get back to school and there will be nothing more there to learn. So I had to weigh the tangible and intangible benefits. Clearly, there is something that's valued in the world market when you can say, 'I went to Harvard Business School' or 'Wharton,' whether you learned anything or not. So I weighed that — the tangibles and the intangibles — to help me evaluate the risk."

Morgan Hall, an operations manager with a Fortune 500 company, talks about the risk of moving out from under her dad's solid reputation in the advertising and PR industry to begin her own business. "I was successful in that I kept my doors open and was profitable. I learned a lot of lessons about running your own business, for one, how difficult it is. But I had clients and I paid my bills. I don't consider it a failure."

Still other risks involve personal decisions with the potential to pull the rug out from under us when we need it the most firmly placed beneath our feet.

Iris Torvik, Ph.D., says, "I think one of the biggest risks I took was when we moved from North Dakota to Oklahoma. Both of our children were just babies, and neither of us had a job. I asked my husband, 'If you could do anything, what would you do?' He wanted to go back to school for a year, and I said, 'Let's go for it.' We felt a real calm about it, and we did that. To everybody else it looked like we were crazy. I got a job within three or four days of arriving in Tulsa, and we were totally taken care of. I think that was the greatest personal risk of all."

Another woman confides her risky decision to leave the emotional security of her home and family: "I was engaged to a doctor. It was going to be the financial security my parents wanted for me. He was older, he was going to make money, and he was wild about me, so there was a lot of emotional security. We'd even set a date, and we were getting so close. I didn't feel much toward him, but I kept thinking about the money, the position, his age, and stability.

"Everybody started talking about us, saying things like, 'You're sure not talking like a new bride.' It was like a business transaction we were discussing. But that goes to show you that other people could see there was no light in me at all, no happiness. I had a brother in Texas and I decided to stay with him awhile, so I could see things clearly. When I was there, I just looked in the want ads and applied for a job. I sent in the resume. [After I returned home] they called me for an interview. I flew back out to Texas and took the job. Then I met my husband. That was a God deal."

Sometimes not to take a risk can be the biggest risk of all.

Jane Brimmer, a senior manager at U.S. West, says, "I was in my late twenties when I took both of my children and moved to Omaha for a job promotion. I had never left home before, but I left the extended family, who are really important in helping you raise children from eastern Iowa. I left it all behind and drove six hours — it felt like 600 hours. It was my first promotion into management. Both my sister and my boss assured me that this was just the beginning step, and through their support I had the courage to do it."

Kathy Darling, corporate vice president with a national retail chain, says, "Marrying my husband was a big risk, because he was twenty-two years older than I was. We'd both been married before, both had children. I had family members who kept telling me that I was making a big mistake — that I shouldn't marry someone who had been married before, who had children, who was so much older. But that was thirty years ago, and we've been very happy ever since."

Sometimes not to take a risk can be the biggest risk of all. Stockbrokers tell us that not to invest our money in stocks is more risky than investing; by keeping money in a low-paying savings account, we risk the likelihood that inflation will eat away its buying potential. The same is often true with risky decisions; not deciding can cost us dearly.

Tough Decisions Resolving Conflict on the Job

According to my interviews with smart women, the toughest decisions — yet the ones we tend to let slide the longest — are those involving conflict on the job. When asked how they were at handling conflict, those surveyed knew where they stood. 55 percent answered that they were good at handling conflict; fifty-five percent said they were uncomfortable and less effective than they wanted to be. Then they went on to describe putting off attempts at resolution for days or decades.

Deciding to get a situation that's not working out in the open and talk about it — even if the other person seems oblivious to the problem — is difficult. Unresolved conflict simply simmers on a back burner and keeps you from moving on to more worthwhile pursuits.

One thing is clear: Indecision about handling conflict causes major stress.

Gail Jones, Ph. D. and program director for the school of medical technology at a major metropolitan hospital, tells about when she put her job on the line to settle a conflict that required a change in the system: "While I was working as a medical technologist, there were only two of us working the night shift. When other people wanted off during other shifts, the person doing the scheduling said they couldn't take off unless he or I agreed to work for them — their shift and ours too — and that just wasn't right. There were other people from other shifts who could work for those wanting off. They even *wanted* to work double shifts for those who wanted to take off. But for some reason, the scheduler decided it had to be one of the two of us from the night shift who worked the double.

"On one occasion, they kept putting pressure on my partner to work a double. They told him if he wanted to keep his job, that was the way it was going to be. When he came back and told me what had happened, I told him that he was my partner. If he didn't have a job there any longer, neither did I, and we would be leaving together. So I went to tell them the situation. Then all of a sudden, within 24 hours, they had very

> *Indecision about handling conflict causes major stress.*

conveniently found some other people to work that shift. That was a risky thing for me then — to put my job on the line for what was right. We weren't close, just coworkers, but it was the right thing to do — a quick decision."

Katy Crane, vice president in charge of new product development for her company, tells of a clash she had with employees over a new product idea. "We had this new product, and I had anticipated a three- to four-month development time. But this project went on for a year and a half. There were so many hurdles. I tried to just keep going, putting one foot in front of the other, believing in the product. I wanted it right. I didn't want to settle for compromise. I just kept pushing and pushing. There was one relationship — and maybe others that I'm unaware of — that has never been the same because I just *insisted* that I was right."

Conflict comes too suddenly, too often, too close to let it cloud our vision, block our goals, and destroy our relationships.

Sheri Nasca, successful realtor with a large national firm, explains her temperament for handling people blocking her path this way: "My grandmother used to say, 'Honey, your success is going to come from your audacity. You're always challenging the moment.' I had then, and have now, little tolerance for an established plan. That's not to say that I always questioned authority or denied respect, but I made that person who was imposing the respect actually earn it."

As little girls, we learned not to create scenes. In resolving any conflict, there is always chance for "a scene." In the workplace, someone's typically watching. That means the other player in the conflict will be tempted to play to the grandstands. No matter. Conflict needs resolution. Otherwise, it can stall your forward motion.

Tough Decisions in Personal Relationships

Some tough decisions come when we are too young; the pressure of the moment — what others will think — looms larger than any future consequence. A friend once told me about her wedding-day dialogue with her dad and her quick decision.

As a young woman, Yvonne had grown up in the lap of luxury and with the social graces that generally accompany money. So when the antithesis of that upbringing came along in a sergeant major with rough edges, she was attracted. Although her family could sense the mismatch that would later turn into a physically abusive relationship, they did not want to deny her this decision. As she later recalled to me, the family could see that the prospective groom was harsh, cold, and insensitive in his treatment of her during their engagement. But she was determined to marry *her* choice, not theirs.

With more than 600 people gathered for their wedding ceremony, she and her dad started down the church aisle. Then her dad turned to her one last time, "Honey, you don't have to go through with this."

She turned and looked up at him, thinking, "Gee, Dad, why didn't you tell me this last night, instead of in front of all these people?" They stopped in the middle of the aisle. She looked around the auditorium at the faces of friends and family, and then said to herself, "I can't...now...," and they kept on walking.

"I will never, ever forget the impact of that moment on my heart."

She recalls to this day: "I will never, ever forget the impact of that moment on my heart. I just wasn't strong enough to face the people who I thought had a different perception of me."

Another interviewee decided differently while there was still time: "I think about one person in particular who was so charming and so courteous and had so much flair. I really forgot a lot of the basics. Momentarily. I had my eyes just on the whipped cream on the sundae, the icing on the cake, and really didn't notice that there was no cake under there. There was no character. The charm and the attentiveness were there, but the basic character was missing. There was a growing sense of 'unpeace.'"

Another looks back: "When I married my ex-husband, I was 19 — very, very young. He was bright, charming, good-looking, the sweep-you-off-your-feet kind. There was something in the "Oh, she's with him" thing. That was a part of it [the attraction]. At the same time I was dating him, I also dated a guy in college who I liked a lot. He was so comfortable. We had so much in common. There was a whole different feeling in being with him. Now, I wonder what would have happened if I had made a different choice at that point in time and could have let go of the Cinderella kind of stuff. What if I had said, 'Here is someone who is a friend, who I like, who I had some romantic feelings for too. I think that things would have been different had I made a different choice."

Other personal decisions and commitments are of an ongoing nature with those we love the most dearly. One respondent shared this: "I've done more 'settling' with my husband this past five years than when we were first married. He's developed a health problem and he has his limitations. His health is more limiting on me than I first thought. After we were married for several years, we had to decide *again* that we were going to *stay* married, that we were going to be good friends. That doesn't mean he is everything that I thought he was going to be when I married him. And I'm sure I'm not everything he thought I was going to be. But we've made the decision to stay together. I'm comfortable with that."

Here's another willful decision in a tough personal situation: "I didn't do any reasoning during the whole process when we met. Those were some of my wild times. After I decided to stop the relationship, I was pregnant. It was too late. We just went ahead and got married because I felt like I couldn't back out. If I had done some processing before, I might not have entered the relationship. But I'll never forget standing there taking my vows — and I wasn't the model Christian teenage girl — I remember thinking, 'I'm not making these vows to Charlie, I'm making them to God.' Standing there, I was thinking this. I knew what the Bible said about vows, and I'd already broken other vows I'd made to God. I felt, for my own peace of mind, that I would not break that vow, and I haven't." This interviewee has now been married for 36 years, and she does not regret standing firm on that decision.

Another smart woman, married for 28 years, confides: "I think there have been times through the years with Roger where I have said, 'If it weren't for the kids, I'm so mad at you now, I would just choose to end this relationship. It would be so much easier to start a new one.' For my part, I'm not sure we would have been married for 28 years without those children. Every once in awhile, there are moments when I'm so mad.... But as I'm sitting here thinking about it, those times are very rare. I have a really deep commitment to him."

Another smart woman made an almost-unheard-of tough decision to leave an abusive marriage temporarily without her children — in order to take care of them permanently in a better situation. "I'm a high risk-taker. I walked out of a physically abusive relationship. I lost my kids. I didn't truly understand the power of money. I officially encountered the sexism in the system and the biases. He literally bought the kids — it's called money under the table. A year later, it all came unraveled, and I stood in the same courtroom and got them back. But it was a huge risk, a big decision."

Another interviewee confides about an unfaithful husband: "The biggest personal decision I've had to make was to believe in my marriage and stand for it when it was looking the worst. People kept telling me to dump him. So it was a risk to myself — to my self-esteem. When somebody leaves you, it really ratchets that low self-esteem. So the tendency was for me to do the tit-for-tat thing, the 'that jerk, I'll show him' thing. It would have been easier to hold my head up and say, 'You're right, this guy's a jerk and I'm going to divorce him and move on.' But I had to stand and say, 'He has hurt me, and I'm going to choose to forgive him. I didn't know how it was going to turn out, but that was my *decision*, my choice. I had to say, 'I'm going to stand and I'm going to bleed for this, not knowing if he will ever come home.' That was a huge risk to my ego." They have now happily been together for over 25 years.

Tough decisions are...well, tough. Right or wrong, there are decisions and commitments that cannot be delegated or relegated to someone else. We can whine, complain, or blame,

Right or wrong, there are decisions and commitments that cannot be delegated or relegated to someone else.

but we cannot drift indefinitely without increasing our own stress and decreasing the options. At one point in their lives, these woman decided to decide, not drift.

Recognize Procrastination and Perform Above Par

Piddling when you think you are paddling is self-delusion. Piddling on purpose is fine. In fact, I have an entire chapter on that in one of my earlier books, *Get a Life Without Sacrificing Your Career.* But when you are piddling around trying to make a go or no-go decision, you are sabotaging your own success.

That is not to say you can't use your subconscious mind to ponder the details. In fact, that's a superior way of coming up with creative alternatives to a difficult situation. We have all had experiences where we are loading the washing machine and all of a sudden we remember the name of the printer who gave us such a good price four years ago on our company brochure. That's our subconscious at work. Purposefully feed your subconscious, and let it work on a problem for you. Load your brain with the facts of a situation, and then give yourself permission to relax and go on about your business until an answer "pops" into your mind.

Set your sites to perform above par routinely.

Unfortunately, the subconscious doesn't come up with all the answers all the time. In those cases, you have to force yourself to focus rather than procrastinate. Bring the situation to the forefront of your mind and focus on it until you decide. Only you know the difference between letting ideas and information germinate and letting yourself off the hook for real results.

Set your sites to perform above par routinely.

You have heard it said that women have to work twice as hard to make half as much as a man in the same job. Thank goodness, according to the most recent research, that's no longer true. Now that women have tenure in the top jobs, the wage gap is disappearing in most professions.

But perform, we must. All of us are having to perform to our fullest capacity in today's environment. With "right sized" organizations, global competition, and lower profit margins, companies expect peak performance from all of us.

Smart women deliver results, not excuses.

Accept Responsibility for Your Decisions

Whether a management decision or a marriage decision, smart women accept responsibility for the outcome of their decisions. They understand the limitations inherent in playing, "No, you decide."

Here is a comment from an interviewee who has come to terms with her own past mistake: "I settled for second best. The marriage didn't last. It took 11 years for it to fail, but we were poorly suited for each other and we knew that from the beginning. Once we got married, I wasn't willing to overlook his shortcomings. I drove him, I pushed him. He was perfectly happy to sit in a $40,000 a year job, and I wanted him to be ambitious. I wanted him to go places and do things with his life. I thought, *He's very talented. He's very witty. He's not good with paperwork, but he has wonderful public speaking skills.* I pushed him unmercifully. It's amazing the marriage held up as long as it did."

As little girls, we listened to mothers and fathers tell us what to do. As elementary-age students, we listened to teachers tell us what to do. As teenagers, we listened to our friends tell us what to do. But at some point, smart women accept responsibility for themselves. They no longer blame others for their weaknesses. They no longer wait for others — parents, husbands or boyfriends, or bosses — to come up with all the answers. They no longer expect others to draw them road maps to find personal satisfaction in their decisions.

Develop Discipline; Don't Discount the Value of Hard Work

With just two albums to her credit, singer Toni Braxton's success has been phenomenal. Her hits have sold more than 11 million copies worldwide and won four Grammys. According to a recent interview with the *Mercury News* in San Jose, California, the singer laughed about her "speed" in

Smart women deliver results, not excuses.

moving up the charts with her new albums. "I'm so blessed. A lot of people say, 'She moved up the ladder really quickly!' But I've been trying a long time. It took me 10 years to get here 'overnight.'"

Madeline Albright has certainly not been selected for the important post of Secretary of State from "out of the blue." From refugee, to professor, to politician, to ambassador, she has practiced patient persistence in realizing her latest goal.

It is rare that any endeavor pays off without patient persistence. Relationships require careful tending. Jobs require due diligence. There are few overnight successes in any endeavor or relationship. Smart women put out the effort, make the hard decisions, take the necessary risks.

Sheri Nasca provides an excellent picture of discipline in a new field. She epitomizes the "young lion," as real estate executives term them, coming into the business with sales ability, computer and Internet savvy, and excellent communication skills. If you know the industry, you know her stats are excellent: She closed $5 million in production in her first nine months. She gets 96.7 percent of her list price and 93 percent of all her listings have sold. Within a few months on the job, she was the top listing agent in her office.

Smart women put out the effort, make the hard decisions, take the necessary risks.

Sheri explains her stellar performance in a completely new-to-her industry this way: "I worked hard. I studied. I watched what the successful agents did. I did my homework. I was up early. I was at the computer before 6:00, before my children even got out of bed. I researched the areas. I researched the companies who were bringing people into the area. I found out who the decision makers were at those companies — who was handling the relocations — and I contacted them. I sent them faxes about potential homes for their executives. I made appointments and called on the vice presidents in those companies. I hand delivered information on appropriate homes to executives who knew other executives that might be moving into the area. On the weekends, I spent my time standing in "open homes" for various builders who had built spec homes. I shook hands with prospective buyers and asked them what they were looking for; then I set about trying to find it for them. I have a passion for personal excellence — following up on the details. I work hard. I am determined."

Smart women exercise self-discipline themselves, and they expect others to do the same. Here's what smart women do differently to accomplish more:

- Feed and exercise their mind.
- Cultivate curiosity.
- Focus and concentrate.
- Avoid trying to complete a project when they have to wait on more information.
- Bunch similar tasks.
- Create systems and processes for the routine so they don't waste energy on rethinking.
- Eliminate the busywork.
- Try not to tell people things they already know.
- Do things right the first time so they don't have to do them over.
- Set priorities.
- Plan.
- Prepare for the worst.
- Organize themselves, their work space, and their information or tools.
- Schedule optimally.
- Work according to their natural rhythm.
- Forget the clock.
- Complete things.
- Delegate completely: the mission, the tangible output, the resources, the deadline, parameters, the worry factors, the checkback points.
- Ask a lot of questions up front.
- Listen to the answers.
- Ask for reasons.
- Refuse to accept excuses.
- Welcome new ideas.
- Question the status quo.
- See obstacles as opportunities.
- Study past mistakes.

Smart women exercise self-discipline themselves, and they expect others to do the same.

- Tame their tongue.
- Say no often.
- Say yes with pleasure.
- Pay attention to detail.
- See the big picture.
- Manage their inventory.
- Hire capable people.
- Hire slowly.
- Fire quickly.
- Pay for quality.
- Watch their nickels and dimes.
- Measure and evaluate their performance.

"Do what you can...every ten minutes," is a favorite motto of one of the survey respondents. If you can't swallow the whole project or responsibility all at once, break it into do-able chunks.

In short, smart women decide, smart women determine, smart women do.

They don't drift.

Practice persistence. Don't do *more* than you can do. But do *all* that you can do. Committing to more than you can do is the surest way to lose your credibility. Doing what you say you will do is the fastest track to confidence — yours and the other person's.

We as women often practice a thorough decision-making process: We gather information, we ask for opinions, we sort the findings. But as in so many other arenas of life, a strength can also be a liability. Our strength as women is that we try to analyze all the details before deciding. Our weakness as women...is that we try to analyze all the details before deciding.

Smart women take the calculated risks, handle confrontation, perform above par, put in the effort, right the wrongs, and deliver the results.

In short, smart women decide, smart women determine, smart women do. They don't drift.

5
Follow Through on Feedback

Several years ago, I was in a studio recording a new audio for release. My assistant, Janet, went along because she is so good at catching my errors. Once in the soundproof room, I began reading aloud from my script. About an hour into the session, she buzzed me to say I had misread a line. I repeated the line. She stopped me again. I repeated the line. She stopped me the third time.

"I'm sorry to keep stopping you, but how are you pronouncing the word," and she spelled it for me, "F - A - C - A - D - E."

I said it again.

She and the technical editor burst out laughing; they began to gesture peculiarly behind the glass wall. The producer stepped inside from the hallway, and then they all three began to laugh convulsively at my expense.

I was puzzled and tired; it wasn't so funny to me. You see, I've heard the word *facade* all my life and have often used it in speaking — it's part of my oral vocabulary. But I'd never connected the oral word to its spelling f-a-c-a-d-e. I guess I had always thought they were two different words meaning the same thing.

And I am supposed to be a communications specialist! Embarrassed? Yes, I was. But the feedback couldn't have been more beneficial. What if I opened a speech someday talking about the FAKADE of personal excellence?

Feedback is invaluable to anyone interested in growth and improvement. According to Publius Syrus: "Many receive advice; few profit by it."

Why? I would guess pride, although I have never done research to support that hypothesis. What I do know is this: There are two kinds of people in the world who hear feedback: Those who respond with, "Hmmm...tell me more" and those who say, "Hmmm...so what makes you so smart?"

We see such reactions daily in our communication courses for corporate clients. One salesperson attending a proposal writing class will approach me at the break and say something like this: "I brought along a personal writing sample, a proposal. When you have time would you review it and give me some feedback?"

"Sure thing," I respond. I review the proposal, add some suggestions for improvements, and return it to the salesperson.

Feedback is invaluable to anyone interested in growth and improvement.

She glances through my comments quickly and says, "Oh, good comments. I'd never thought of doing what you suggested on page 6. And you're exactly right, I agree that there's too much detail here. And, yeah, I see your point here on page 8 about uninformative headings. This is very helpful. Thank you. I'll use your comments on the next proposal."

Then there are the people from the other group: A salesperson attending the class will approach me at break with a proposal. "Would you glance over this proposal and give me your comments."

"Sure thing," I respond. I review the proposal, add some suggestions for improvements, and return it to the salesperson.

She glances through my comments and says, "Hmmm. Well, it got me the business anyway — $2 million. It couldn't be all that bad, right?"

What's the difference between these two typical reactions to feedback: Attitude. Open or closed for business.

Know the Difference Between Feedback and Advice

The advice we receive from others tends to be largely

our own; we hint at what we want others to tell us. Writer John Steinbeck insists, "No one wants advice — only corroboration."

Feedback, on the other hand, often is the label we attach to those negative comments we receive from both loved ones and outsiders. To be successful in love and life, women need both kinds of comments to help them chart a successful, fulfilling life.

Let's talk about advice for a moment. A successful company has advisers; we call them the board of directors. Successful individuals have advisers; we call them mentors, coaches, or friends. In our jobs, we realize the benefit of having advisers, but somehow we neglect that same issue in our personal lives. When we have a problem disciplining our teenage son or when we can't decide about going back to school at midlife, we often fail to seek and profit from usable advice.

Successful individuals have advisers; we call them mentors, coaches, or friends.

If you want helpful advice — advice that's not your own — you have to shop around. You have to determine who has the insight or expertise you need. In other words, who are your best resources for what specific kind of information? If you want advice about handling a toddler's toilet training, ask other mothers or a doctor. If you want advice about starting your own small business, ask someone who has done it. If you want advice about pesticides for your lawn, ask someone who works in a plant nursery. If you want advice about raising money to start your own business, talk to a CPA or a venture capitalist.

Sounds simple enough, doesn't it? But when we get into stressful situations and realize we need help, we often ask opinions from anyone who happens to be handy rather than someone qualified to know. We ask singles about what makes a happy marriage. We ask football coaches about team building within a corporation. We ask cab drivers for stock tips. We ask our sister-in-law whether our newly drafted living will looks legal. Yet, step number one in receiving helpful advice is seeking the right people as resources.

How you ask for advice also makes a great deal of

difference in the soundness of the advice you receive. For example: "My son is really having difficulties in school. His teachers say he can't sit still and pay attention, and our doctor has suggested that we try him on some medication for hyperactivity. But I'm afraid to start that routine, because there are so many side effects. Marilyn's little girl was on that medication, and it just made her worse. I think Timmy would be better off without it. What do you think?"

Now if you were the neighbor listening to this mother, what kind of comment or advice do you think she wants? Exactly. Agreement and affirmation that she's doing the right thing. The two women would have to be very close friends for the listener to give her an opposing opinion at this point.

But what if the mother had phrased her comments this way: "Timmy's having trouble in school. His teachers say he's hyperactive and can't pay attention. Our family doctor wants to put him on medication, but I'm confused. Do you know anyone else who has been diagnosed as hyperactive? Are you aware of any dangerous side effects to that medication?"

This alternative phrasing would more likely lead to more helpful advice and information.

In general, it's better to tell your potential adviser the *kind* of advice you want. Do you need hard-core facts from them? Their opinions? Personal experience? Do you want them to listen for gaps in your own reasoning and logic? Do you want them to help you list the pros and cons of a situation before you make a decision? Or, do you simply want support and encouragement on what you have already decided to do?

Focus on what kind of comments you want from your advisers. Otherwise, you will get a lot of useless advice and waste your time and theirs in the process.

Frequently I receive calls from other members in my professional association, asking something like this: "I was just thinking about writing a book. Could you tell me how to get started?" Always puzzled by that global question, I have to ask them a series of prompts to discover what they really want to know. For example, do they want to know how to organize and format their ideas? How to get a literary agent? How to find a publisher? How to do research? How to negotiate a big advance and a good contract? How to promote the book?

To make matters worse, when I ask them these series of prompt questions, I get something like this: "Yeah, I want to know all of that."

Running through my mind is the question: "In two minutes or less, or do you have all day?" Entire books have been written on each of those issues. You can understand the complexity of trying to offer something really helpful, when the other person hasn't focused on what he or she needs to know.

On the other hand, I love to help callers with specific questions like, "My book idea is x. Which publisher do you think would be the best to market and promote this kind of book in a big way?" I can deal with a specific question much more effectively.

Specific, focused questions to the right people will solicit helpful, usable advice.

Let's say you are thinking of beginning your own graphics design business and need some help. To a friend who has just started his or her own business, you might ask, "How did you go about selecting a company name?" "What drawbacks do you experience in having a home office?" "Where's an inexpensive place to buy business cards and stationery?"

To a friend who's a computer whiz, you might ask: "What software package do you use for graphics?" "What are the most important criteria in selecting a graphics package?"

To another mother who works outside the home, you might ask, "My children are going to have to stay at home alone in the afternoons about thirty minutes before I get home. What rules have you found helpful in keeping them safe and entertained in your absence?

Specific, focused questions to the right people will solicit helpful, usable advice. On the other hand, global, vague questions will elicit only blank stares and useless information.

Most people *say* they welcome usable advice, but too often they actually discard negative comments — and with great pain and a sense of being "done wrong." According to Will Rogers, "A remark generally hurts in proportion to its truth." Yet, we set about trying to prove to ourselves and others that the observation is false.

When I started back to college for my master's degree, I enrolled in a creative writing class. Every class session we would bring poems, short stories, and novel chapters to class to read and to be critiqued by our classmates and our professor. On the last night of class, I said to my professor, "I want your honest feedback on my writing abilities. You've heard my work this semester. For most of these people in this class, writing is just a hobby, a course elective. But I'm dead serious. I've just quit my job to become a full-time writer. So would you just give me your honest opinion about my work this semester?"

The professor stared at the floor for what seemed like forever, then finally looked up: "Dianna,...novel writing...isn't for everyone."

So what did I do? I spent the next two years of my life trying to write novels to prove her wrong! Later when my first novel came out, I felt the urge to send her a copy and say, "See there!" But I had the wrong attitude back then. That professor was right — nonfiction is my real gift. But that realization came only after I had wasted two years of effort because I was unwilling to accept feedback.

You have heard it said about bad breath: "Even your best friends won't tell you." The same often proves to be true when it comes to useful but negative feedback. Most people won't find it easy to give honest feedback.

Take the Initiative

Many people mistakenly assume that feedback from coworkers and bosses will be forthcoming. Not so. Like friends, managers are generally poor at giving usable feedback — even positive feedback. They often don't tell you exactly what you did to get the good rating, so you don't know exactly what to repeat next time. They hate to hurt feelings when the feedback is negative, so they seldom think to tell you about their expectations. They often assume you know. Yet women continue to stake their careers and jobs on a boss's ability and willingness to give feedback.

A soon-to-be executive at Exxon, during a consulting situation on presentation skills, answered one of my initial questions in diagnosing his difficulties with this comment: I asked him, "Have you ever received any comments, either positive or negative, from a boss or peer about your presentation skills?" He looked at me pensively and then responded, "Never. But come to think of it, I guess that should tell me a lot. If I'm good, they wouldn't hesitate to point that out, right? Most people dread to point out weaknesses, so they don't say anything."

He was correct in his observations. His boss had shared with me that if he couldn't get some help, his upward mobility would soon come to a screeching halt.

Don't leave a supervisor or team leader an option. Take the initiative in getting feedback. You have too much to lose if you don't get feedback and much to gain if you do.

What's wrong with making an appointment with your boss or committee chair and asking for feedback on recent projects? Ask things like: "What did you think went well with this last project? What suggestions would you have for doing things differently next time?" And in general, periodically ask, "What things do you most value in my performance and skill set? What's lacking? What other skills do you think people in my job should acquire?"

This generalized wording gives supervisors a way to talk anonymously about "people in this position in general" versus *you* specifically. Then you can make the judgment about how your attitudes, skills, and habits match what your boss values. It works. If you want feedback from a boss, you can get it. You just have to take the initiative.

The difficulty in getting helpful feedback doesn't lessen the importance of the effort. Corporations around the world are helping their employees seek and evaluate performance by giving them opportunities for what's called "360 degrees feedback." That means that not only does the supervisor give

You have too much to lose if you don't get feedback and much to gain if you do.

his or her employees performance appraisals, but employees also rate their supervisors and coworkers.

How about at home? Are husbands any more willing to give feedback than bosses? Well, that depends. Spouses hate to give negative feedback because they fear creating a distance in the relationship. They don't want to hurt the relationship, so they just keep quiet about personality quirks and behaviorial issues that perhaps need to be changed.

Children, for the most part, hold their tongues also on the "heavy" feedback. Why? They're in a position to be punished for what they say, for hurting your feelings.

Yes, of course, spouses and children do have negative comments for us. But those negatives usually come out in a moment of anger over a particular situation. As listeners, we often shrug those comments aside, without giving full weight to them because of the associated anger. Wrong move! A more beneficial response would be to sift the nuggets of truth from the comments before blowing away the wrappings of anger.

Friends and acquaintances also hesitate to give us negative feedback for several reasons: 1) They don't think they know us well enough. 2) They don't feel responsible for our personal growth. 3) They don't care enough about us. 4) They don't want to create hard feelings and ruin a smooth relationship.

As a result, we never get valuable feedback that could help us immeasurably at home and at work.

For example, just recently we built a new home. Needless to say, there were some glitches. As we moved through the process, I noted frustrations that could have been avoided had the builder and his crews done things a little differently. For example, following their schedule of meetings and selection decisions, they had us decide on floor and shower tiles in the bathroom before we selected wallpaper. To me, the hardest selections in building a house involve finding wallpaper with the appropriate colors for the right rooms. I would like to have selected the wallpaper first, and then have chosen the floor and shower tile to match.

Many similar decisions created frustration and rework for both us and the subcontracting crews. Did I tell the builder my ideas for improving the construction process for all concerned? No. Why not? His attitude.

When I started to mention one particular part of the process that seemed to be done in reverse order, he commented, "Look, we don't build a perfect house." The underlying meaning was, "We know our business; we're closed to others' observations and ideas." As a customer, I withheld valuable information that might have made the builder's process much simpler for him and future home buyers.

Contrary to what most people think, helpful feedback doesn't come to us easily, and one of the surest marks of character is the willingness to accept negative feedback without feeling animosity toward the person who gave it. Tough, but possible.

...one of the surest marks of character is the willingness to accept negative feedback without feeling animosity toward the person who gave it.

Consider Negative Feedback a Gift, Not a Gripe

Peter Drucker, professor and management consultant, traces the process of keeping himself intellectually alive back to prolonged sessions of critique with an editor-in-chief at one of Europe's leading newspapers back in the 1930s. That editor-in-chief took infinite pains to train and discipline his journalism crew. Twice a year, he would spend an entire weekend discussing their work for the previous six months.

They started the sessions with what they had done well, then moved to what they had tried to do well, and ended with things they hadn't done well enough. After he subjected them to what Drucker calls "scathing critiques" of what they had failed to do or had done badly, they focused on how to correct the work and improve their skills during the next six months. A week after these feedback sessions, Drucker and the other two journalists had to give the editor their plans for learning during the next six months.

Drucker recalls, "Almost ten years later, after I had come to the United States, I remembered them. It was in the early 1940s, after I had become a senior professor, started my own consulting practice, and begun to publish major books. Since then I have set aside two weeks every summer in which to review my work during the preceding year, beginning with the things I did well but could or should have done better, down to the things I did poorly and the things I should have done but did not do. I decide what my priorities should be in my consulting work, in my writing, and in my teaching. I have never once truly lived up to the plan I make each August, but it has forced me to live up to Verdi's injunction to strive for perfection, even though 'it has always eluded me' and still does."

From the quality of Drucker's contribution to modern management in the United States, we understand the value of that feedback to him as a young journalist.

Unfortunately, the rest of us don't always welcome "scathing critique," or even kind, "constructive feedback." Attitude — ours and the other person's — makes all the difference.

The mental trick is thinking of negative feedback as a gift, not a gripe.

The mental trick is thinking of negative feedback as a gift, not a gripe. Someone in one of my audiences once got my attention with that "gift" label. I had just used an illustration in one of my speeches about a dying child. Although I don't remember the point I was making at the time, I do remember a woman who walked up to me after the session and said, "I want to give you a gift — some feedback."

"Okay," I said, bracing for an attack, not fully expecting that I'd consider it a "gift" after she finished with me.

She continued, "I noticed that when you told the story about the dying child you caused pain for Morgan. I don't know if you are aware or not, but she has a very sick child, and I could just see her eyes mist over while you were talking."

It was a valuable reminder for me. Of course, I can't always know the circumstances of every member of a large audience, but her larger issue was sensitivity to all, whether the issue is ethnicity, gender, faith, or tragedy. I agree — the reminder was a gift.

Considering negative feedback as a gift is a tall order

sometimes, particularly when that feedback comes from someone you don't necessarily like or respect.

One interviewee talked about how often her ex-husband gave her advice about how to handle their teenage son. The boy's father kept telling her that she didn't communicate with her son, that she just insisted on "telling him how things should be, without listening to his viewpoints." After swallowing her pride and evaluating the situation, she says, "It was hurtful to me. I resisted it a long time. I didn't realize I was doing that. But I took it to heart, and it has really made a difference. Our relationship has improved."

Here are other feedback comments that interviewees have come to think of as "gifts."

From a middle manager: "There were some times in life that I've had people share that their perception of me was that I cared more about getting the job done than about the people that were on the team. They said that in my effort to "make it happen," I came across as aloof. Through some later training and personality typing, I've come to understand how to read people better. I've realized that my tasks are really very dependent on other people."

From a director of nursing: "About fifteen years ago, one of the new natologists here told me that I was an excellent bedside nurse, but that I would never make it in management because I wasn't assertive enough. That was a real challenge to me, because I felt that I had something to offer in leadership. I felt that I could be fair, unbiased, and could be a voice to speak up for women here. I believe in finding mentors, and I studied leadership. I read a lot of Covey principle-centered leadership. We have to choose to be mentored."

An actress tells about a long growth curve in her inability to trust her own creativity: "I had a screen test for a soap opera. I was down to the screen test, after having gone through several preliminary auditions with the casting director. Five women were being screened for this role. We got the script ahead of time, but I have a tendency to overprepare. I thought, *I'm gonna know the words, but I don't want to kill it with memorization.* So I show up and get blocking with a director. That's the movement of the scene. Then I did the blocking of that movement for the camera with the lights and everything, sort of like a dress rehearsal. Then one by one, they called the women in for the screen test. I was alone in that huge sound studio with the other actor who had already gotten the other role. He's on the series now.

"And I blew it. I was so anxious about getting all that blocking right and all my movements exactly that I forgot the most important thing — to be myself and put myself into the situation. I didn't get the job, and it just crushed me. But I feel like I know why. Rather than feeling strong in my own creativity, I tried to second guess what other people wanted. I try not to do that anymore."

From an executive in product development: "I'm a feeler, so if something is goofy, I tend to think it's my fault. If the meeting has gone badly, it's probably because I was there. One of the things I'm working on now is self-centeredness. People tend to think of self-centeredness as pride and ego and wanting your own way. That's one side of it. But for me, there is another side, which is indulging yourself in pity parties. Assuming I was the problem in a meeting like that is a form of self-centeredness. It's like you're just stuck on yourself and you're just spiraling in and spending all this time on yourself. I used to think it was because I was in a man's world in upper management. There were times I thought it was because I was a woman. But I've come to realize it was just self-centeredness on my part."

When given the gift of feedback, smart women take it to heart.

We've all heard the old saying, "A lesson is repeated until you learn it." Likewise, feedback is often repeated until you learn it. When given the gift of feedback, smart women take it to heart.

As With Medicine, Apply Liberally to the Affected Area

After you receive feedback, of course, you have to learn to analyze and evaluate it in light of your personal values and goals. Here are a few filters that may be helpful:

- Do I really understand this comment — what is the real

issue, point, or message?

- Am I being overly sensitive?
- Am I being too cavalier?
- Is this person in a position to know what he/she is talking about?
- Is there any other evidence to support the same viewpoint?
- Do I *want* to be different or act differently?
- If I don't need to make changes, how can I change this person's perception of me or what I did or am about to do?

Sometimes those questions will keep you from going off the proverbial deep-end on feedback that's wrong, inappropriate, and limiting to your potential.

One interviewee recalls being momentarily taken back with a friend's feedback about her decision to go to work with a large seminar company early in her career. Her friend counseled: "You can't do that. They'll never hire a black woman to do that. They don't have black trainers. You're wasting your time." Speaker Hattie Hill also remembers filtering that feedback through her own "Rules for Life." "I listened. And it did slow me down — for the night. I thought it over and then I reasoned, *Well, if they don't have one [black trainer], they need one. I'm still going to try.* Friends who say those things are trying to help — they don't want you to get hurt. But you have to decide for yourself if you buy that feedback."

Another interviewee tells about her experience in filtering feedback from a subordinate. Executive Ann-Marie Stephens says, "I had this one person who reported to me, and his attitude to me was always, 'I'd never do your job the way you're doing it.' But I had to do a little thinking about what was driving him. He had been passed over for promotion several times. I had the job he wanted. So I had to say to him, 'When you get this job, part of having the job will be that you can do it the way you'd like to do it. Right now, it's my job, this is how I like to do it, and things seem to be working fine, thank you. You have to draw the line between opinions that are valid and welcome and those that don't have merit."

Smart thinking from both women. Filter questions and feedback go hand in hand. Your mission is to sift the reflective from the flaky.

A client of mine, who manages 45 employees at a large telecommunications company, told me recently about a former boss she admired greatly. Jane had been hired to turn around a division of the company that had been losing money for several years. When she accepted the job, she began to revolutionize the way they did business. She shuffled people into new jobs, replaced old equipment, changed the marketing strategies, raised prices, and trained her salespeople more efficiently on the product. As a result, she surpassed the company's profit expectations for her division.

When her boss called her in for her annual performance appraisal, Jane enjoyed the litany of successes her manager mentioned. Then when the manager got to the "Action Needed" section of the evaluation form, she said to Jane: "In our 360-degree feedback process, your employees have said you're judgmental and opinionated. Do you want to do anything about it?"

Filter questions and feedback go hand in hand. Your mission is to sift the reflective from the flaky.

Over dinner with me, Jane laughed about the incident in her distant past: "I loved the way my boss phrased it, 'Do you want to do anything about it?' She provided the feedback and left the initiative up to me about whether I wanted to make changes. And, you know, in light of my goals during that first year in the new job, I didn't want to do anything about it. I had made quick judgments and had been opinionated about changes that needed to be made. I wasn't working to be crowned Miss Easy-Going. My goal was to improve profitability."

Jane, since that time, has worked on being less opinionated. But she initially used that feedback in light of her own goals. Smart move.

Sometimes the feedback can turn into a high-dollar commodity immediately. Chris had worked in our office for several years when she decided that she needed more money than she was currently earning. She sat down with me and explained: "I've got two teenage sons who'll need college tuition in about three to four years. I've got to find a way to make more money. I need at least a $5,000 raise."

"You've done excellent work this year," I responded. "We appreciate your efforts very much, but we just can't afford a $5,000 raise. We're going to have to hire a new trainer and buy a new copier."

"But the company's done well this year."

"You're right. We have. But you're at the top of your field, making as much as any executive secretary. We as a company have to decide how much those duties are worth. The salary you're making is maximum for the value of that position."

Chris started to cry. "What am I going to do? I've got to have more money. I guess I'll just update my resume and start looking elsewhere."

My first reaction was to panic and agree to the raise that I knew we couldn't afford and that would put a big dent in our other plans. She did an excellent job for us, we worked well together, and from my knowledge of her situation at home, I agreed that she probably did need more money. I wanted to help.

To her obvious surprise, I said, "That's a good idea — although we'd hate to lose you. I have a suggestion. Have you thought about changing careers? Have you thought about repackaging your secretarial skills and looking for a job with a different label — say, training coordinator? You'd be using the same skills, but with a different end product — a course manual. I've noted your creativity in training our new people on the computers."

No, she admitted that she hadn't thought of that. She'd never thought of entering the training field at all. But two days later, she had an updated resume and a new goal. Two months later, she had a new job as training coordinator for a hospital, earning almost twice her secretarial salary. Smart move for her. And I'd like to think she still appreciates my coaching!

Queue Up with Smart Questions

Advice and feedback from an unbiased, qualified source

can be invaluable. Just remember always to evaluate the feedback you receive in light of your own goals, not someone else's goals for your life.

If your mother-in-law comments that you're a lousy housekeeper, and your goal is not to keep an immaculate house, then you can ignore that feedback. If your son quips about your lack of know-how in hooking up the new stereo system, and if becoming a mechanical wizard isn't one of your personal goals, let the comment pass.

Feedback — both positive and negative — can provide both direction and motivation. In your own life, determine where you could use some unbiased feedback.

As a spouse, ask these questions:

Feedback — both positive and negative — can provide both direction and motivation.

- What can I do to make you feel more loved and appreciated?
- What needs of yours am I meeting?
- What needs of yours am I not meeting?
- What could I do to strengthen the intimacy between us?
- What goals do you have that I could help you work toward?

As a mother, ask these questions:

- How do you know I love you?
- In what ways could I show you more support and love?
- How interested do I seem in your schoolwork?
- How interested do I seem in your social life?
- If there were such a thing as a perfect parent, what else would I need to learn before I could become one?
- If you had a wish about our relationship, what would that wish be?

As a friend, ask these questions:

- How would you describe a good friend?
- In what ways can you count on me as a friend?
- In what ways have I let you down as a friend?
- If you had a wish about our friendship, what would it be?

As an employee/employer, ask these questions:

- What are my key strengths on the job?
- What are my key weaknesses on the job?

- What skills, traits, or attitudes would the ideal employee in my job have?
- The next time I do another project similar to the one I just finished, what would you like to see me do differently?
- How can I better help you meet your needs and goals?
- What in my attitude and personality am I unaware of that might be harmful to my career advancement?
- What about my attitude and personality will be most advantageous in my career advancement?

And when you get answers, follow through.

We need to measure ourselves with someone else's yardstick occasionally. If your spouse says you're irritable, and your kids say you're irritable, and your colleagues say you're irritable, then chances are...you're irritable. If you're getting the same feedback from several sources, pay attention. What action can you take to improve in that area?

It's strange that we're often willing to pay big bucks to a doctor or psychologist for her feedback, but hesitant in seeking free feedback. And feedback from those who are close enough to know us well is often discounted the most.

Smart women take the initiative in getting feedback at work and at home.

Feedback, properly evaluated, from a caring contributor, can be invaluable in gaining perspective on where you're going, what you're doing, and what kind of person you're becoming. Smart women take the initiative in getting feedback at work and at home. They follow through on filtering and applying that feedback to reach their goals. Feedback costs, but feedback pays.

6
Entertain Only Ethical Choices

bout four years ago I decided to redecorate my home. I had about three parties coming up in a two-month period, plus my parents' fiftieth wedding anniversary celebration, and the house needed a facelift anyway. On a recommendation from an acquaintance, I called an interior decorator in Dallas and asked if she could come out to meet with me. She did. After a quick walk-through, she made a few suggestions and invited me into her shop to select fabric for a sofa and three chairs.

The following week in her shop, we had been huddled over the fabric swatches about five minutes, when a male customer at her counter thundered, "I want someone to give me a refund on that chair NOW. I've been waiting half an hour and I mean NOW!" The owner-decorator peered up over the selection books slowly. Then, "We're busy. You can just wait another half hour if that's what it takes."

That should have been an omen to me that all was not well, but I shrugged off the scene and gave the decorator the benefit of the doubt. After all, there was such a thing as obnoxious customers, and I didn't know the whole story.

An hour later, she and I had selected fabric for the custom pieces, and she promised to fax the prices after she figured the yardages. When the quote came, her prices were a little higher than she'd estimated "off the cuff" in the store. Did she include her fee in these estimates? I was unclear, so

I phoned her.

"I don't charge a fee, per se. My advice and time are compensated for in the margin I make on the items you buy through my own shop."

"But you mentioned some accessories — the lamps and cocktail tables, those dining chairs, some pictures, and a few knick-knacks — those won't be purchased through your shop?"

"Yes, but shopping for the other things won't take long. I'm in the Trade Center every day or two, and I'll keep my eyes open. I give them so much volume that I can usually get a better price than the customer can directly. It'll just take us an hour or two. I figured my time into the sofa and chairs we're doing for you."

Sounded reasonable to me. I okayed the estimate she'd faxed for the sofa and chairs, and they began the project.

A week later, she phoned me to meet her at Haverty's, where she'd located the lamps, cocktail tables, and dining chairs to match my old table. We agreed on the selections, and she sent me on my way back to my office with, "Okay, I'll negotiate with the manager tomorrow night when I'm back in here again. I'm in a hurry now. I'll fax you their best price."

Sounded reasonable to me. I left the bargaining in her hands and returned to work. Two days later, she faxed the estimate. Again, the pricing was a good bit higher than expected.

The following Saturday my husband and I unexpectedly drove through Ft. Worth and happened to see another Haverty's store. "Let's stop and let me show you what the decorator selected." Surprise! The dining chairs were all on sale 20 percent off and 20 percent less than the price the decorator had faxed to me on Thursday. That's strange. I thought she told me she could get them at a deep discount. Well, maybe she decided to add something else for her "shopping fee" after all.

The following Monday I phoned her store and left her a voice mail: "I happened to be in Haverty's Ft. Worth store Saturday and found the dining chairs and lamps we looked at in Dallas. They're on sale! And with that sale, they're even cheaper than the discounted prices you faxed to me. Is the extra cost included in the faxed estimate your shopping fee? I understood you to say you were not adding anything extra to the cost of these items because you were making your money on the furniture I ordered through your own store. Is that correct? Please get back to me right away because the sale goes off today!"

She didn't return the call. On Wednesday when she still hadn't returned the call, I phoned Haverty's in Dallas to talk to the manager. Could he verify the quotes from his store to the decorator? He did. They were much lower than what the decorator had faxed to me.

When I again phoned the decorator's to ask for an explanation, she pretended surprise at the "mix-up."

"Look, if you can get the lamps and dining chairs cheaper yourself, just go ahead and buy them." She sounded very perturbed. "I faxed you the same price that the Dallas manager gave me. I've added nothing for my fee."

"Well, there's a mix-up somewhere, but never mind. I'll go ahead and buy the lamps and dining chairs myself. I think Haverty's will still give me the sale price. But what about the pictures and other accessories you were going to help me select at the Trade Center? You said it would take us about an hour some day at lunch."

"I'll have to check my schedule and get back to you."

"Okay, that's fine. But I really need to do it this week. Remember the fiftieth wedding anniversary celebration and a houseful of guests will be arriving Saturday."

"I remember."

"So you'll call back so we can select the accessories this week?"

"Yes. We'll make it Tuesday or Wednesday afternoon. I'll check my calendar and call you."

I waited. She didn't call.

I phoned again. "When are we going to shop for the accessories? The anniversary party is Saturday."

"No problem. We'll go Thursday night. I'll phone late

Thursday afternoon to tell you what time."

She didn't call Thursday. I phoned again Friday morning. She answered, "The delivery people will be there this morning with the sofa and two chairs. One chair didn't come in."

"Okay, but what about the accessories?"

"I've already got things picked out that I know you'll love. It'll only take us an hour. I'll meet you at the house with them when they deliver the furniture to make sure they set everything in the right spot."

Later in the day, the delivery people show up; the decorator does not. The delivery man has this message, "Gail said to tell you she had something come up. She'll phone in the morning and meet you to show you her selections and then come out here to help you hang the pictures."

"My parents' anniversary party is tomorrow! Our guests will be here then!"

"That's all I know, ma'am. She just said to tell you that she'll be here in the morning."

Smart women never jeopardize their integrity

On Saturday at noon, with all my naiveté still intact, I finally understood that she did not intend to call back about the accessories. The scene with the angry customer demanding a refund on that first day in her shop flashed back. She had made her profit on the furniture purchased in her shop, had almost made a second profit through the Haverty's selections, and didn't intend to spend any more time fulfilling her related shopping commitments.

Hurriedly, I dashed out to make the last few selections on my own before the guests rang my doorbell. I never heard from the decorator again, and the last time I drove through her area of Dallas, her shop had vanished.

Such unethical dealings ruin businesses. But they also ruin people.

Character Counts, and Perception Can Penalize

Smart women never jeopardize their integrity. Smart women know that businesses come and go. Jobs come and go. Situations come and go. Dollars come and go. In the best of times and in the worst of times, all that stands between opportunity and disaster is character. In the marketplace, in the community, and in social circles, character counts.

Even at the bank. Sure, it does! When loan officers approve or refuse loans, they consider the 5 Cs of credit decisions: credit history, capacity, collateral, cash flow, and character. Character — even an outsider's assessment of character — makes a difference whether you get a loan, get a job, or get a bill.

As I interviewed the successful entrepreneurs for this book, they all insisted that for the long haul, one's integrity had to be beyond question.

What kind of character issues place women in jeopardy? The list is long, but I would say that close to the top is sexual behavior. If a successful woman looks good, some people still assume that she got where she is because of sexual favors. If she is not particularly good-looking, some people assume that she is so desperate that she will welcome sexual encounters whenever they come her way.

Perception can be the most damaging part of the whole situation. It's not what happened or happens, but what people *think* happened or happens that makes a difference.

I learned a lot about perception from one such incident at age 30. I had just begun my consulting and training business when I landed one of the smaller gas pipeline companies in Houston as a client.

I arrived in Kansas City to conduct a technical writing class for the client. My client contact picked me up at the hotel the morning of the first day of the training class, and as we drove to the company site, he explained, "Just want to give you the inside scoop on our company. You probably know that the oil-and-gas industry is a good-old-boy network."

I nodded. No surprise to anybody who had lived in Houston more than a few weeks.

"Socializing is really important. Just wanted to let you know that these guys party, and if you're going to be successful here and win their confidence in the classroom, you're going to have to be 'one of the guys' outside the classroom."

In the marketplace,

in the community,

and in social circles,

character counts.

"O...kay," I said, eager to catch on during my first trip out of town on business. He sounded like a big brother trying to let me in on the secrets of how the big bad world really operated. Being new to the whole business scene (right out of graduate school), I was eager to learn. Although I wasn't quite sure what "being one of the guys" entailed, I felt confident that I could talk good-old-boy in the hallways at break if necessary.

My contact continued, "As soon as you dismiss class at five, they're going to head for the bar in the hotel. Even if you don't drink, I would suggest you make an appearance in the bar. Sit around and visit with them and go out to dinner. We all get together to go out somewhere, and I suggest you come along. You'll be the only woman, but I hope that won't matter."

"Sure, no problem. That sounds fine," I tried to reassure him. His credibility was on the line because he'd hired me, and therefore whatever I did or didn't do would reflect on him. I wanted him to know that he'd made the right decision, that I could be a good-old-boy.

"They do business with people they like," he repeated.

"I understand. I don't think it'll be a problem."

When I dismissed the engineers and their managers at five o'clock, they all headed for the bar, as predicted. I followed suit.

I sat there and talked while they drank and swapped stories and information from their various regions. Finally, about seven, the senior-ranking vice president suggested that we "go find a place to eat" and invited me to join them. Several of them, including me, said they needed to stop back by their rooms to grab a jacket, so the VP suggested we all meet back in the lobby in ten minutes and then decide where to eat dinner.

When I returned to the appointed spot in the lobby, they were huddled in two groups on opposite sides of the hallway. The vice president, flanked by about six guys, said, "Well, we decided we'd just stay here for dinner. The restaurant looks pretty good. You want to join us?"

"That sounds fine." I started to walk in his direction.

But then the second voice called from behind me. "Or, had you rather go out with us? We're going to a steak house down the road. Some of us are tired of staying in all day. It's nice outside, if you'd like to join us?"

"Well, that sounds good too."

I looked back to the vice president and then back to the guy and his group making the last invitation. Which way to go? Who outranked whom? Did that matter? Who was this other guy anyway? I couldn't remember his name or title. I stood frozen for a moment, and then the thought of another of their round of drinks at the bar after dinner flashed through my mind. I really did want to get to bed early for the next day, so I decided the group leaving the hotel would probably make it a quicker evening. "Okay," I finally stammered an answer, "A bit of fresh air would be a nice change. I'll opt for the steak house, I guess."

The vice president shrugged, and his group headed into the restaurant off the hallway.

The crowd I was following dispersed into several cars, and the man who'd offered the invitation said, "Here, my car is over here." I followed him to his rental car, and we waited a few moments. "Guess no one else is riding with us," he said. So we backed out of the parking lot and headed for the steak house by ourselves. Once inside, I wondered aloud, "What happened to everybody else? I thought they were all coming along?"

"Don't know," he said. "Maybe they changed their minds. Or, maybe we miscommunicated on the place. Anyway, I'm hungry. Let's go ahead and order." More than a little concerned, I ordered. No one else ever showed up. We ate, and then we returned to the hotel. I walked through the lobby, saw no one on my way in, and went straight to my room for an early night.

The next morning when I arrived at the training room, no one mentioned dinner, so neither did I. The vice president seemed a little cool, so I thought I'd probe a little with my client contact. I asked, "So what did you do for dinner last night?"

"Went down the street to a place — I forget the name of it."

"Well, I thought there was a group of us going to a steak house, but nobody else ever showed up — just Bill and I. You know what happened to the rest?"

"Don't know." He grew quiet again.

"So," I continued to probe, "Who stayed and ate here in the restaurant?"

"Dirk and a few others, I don't know for sure. I told you he was the vice president, didn't I?" I nodded. "I think his feelings were a little hurt."

"At me?"

He nodded.

"Well, I never thought — Bill just said a group was going out to get steak, and I didn't know—"

"I think he took it as a personal affront in front of the others."

"But —"

Someone else walked up and we changed the subject.

Perception and appearances ruled the day.

At the end of the class day, the attendees' evaluations were exceptionally good and I breathed a sign of relief. I wrote my customary thank-you letter to the client contact and didn't hear from him for a few months. When I got around to calling him about four months later to talk about future classes, he said he didn't plan to schedule another class. No further business, no further explanation.

About a year later, I phoned again to learn there was another person in the job — one of the attendees in the first workshop. He offered this explanation: "I think word got around — probably through Bill's brag — that you and he spent the evening together. I think the vice president was a little offended that you didn't decide to have dinner with him."

My explanation of the evening didn't matter at that point. Perception and appearances ruled the day. Eventually, we did rebook work for this client, but it was several years down the road.

It only took one such incident for me to learn the mine-field that surrounds anyone in the workplace. In the intervening eighteen years, things have changed — but not all that much. Today, the sexual pressure flows both ways, men making unwanted advances and leaving innuendoes and women enticing and falsely accusing men.

Sexual harassment situations represent only a part of the ethical issues that we all face every day. One attorney interviewee talks about the ethics of how to handle a court case in an ethical way: "There were a couple of different ways to try the case. The more 'sensitive' way or the brutal way. I chose what I thought was the better way. It paid off. The jury found in our favor. The client had wanted us to bloody the other side, and we chose not to do that. We risked really upsetting our client — not trying the case the way they wanted it handled, but they were happy in the end."

However, not all ethical predicaments turn out with everyone living happily ever after. The bad guys and gals don't always lose and the good guys and gals don't always win.

Several years ago, Judith Briles put together a group of investors to buy a small hotel. She and her investors were victims of an embezzlement, in which the hotel eventually had to declare bankruptcy. Others involved washed their hands as they left the sinking ship, but Judith tried to stay and protect the money invested by her colleagues. She says: "That hotel was one of the reasons I went back to get my doctorate. I had to learn how to run a hotel. During the two years that I was working on my doctorate, every paper I worked on dealt with some transitional phase we were in at the hotel. If I had been able to do the projections at the beginning — as I later learned to do — I would have known from the beginning that all would have ended in disaster, no matter how hard I tried to pull it all together and save the situation. In the end, the creditors got 100 cents on the dollar, which you know with any bankruptcy is a good deal. All the creditors got their money back. All the investors lost theirs. But I tried to stay with it and do the right thing. It destroyed over ten years of our lives financially."

Watch for Forks in the Road, and Know Which Way You Intend to Turn Before You Get There

Winning or losing, bounty or bankruptcy is not the point. Doing the right thing is. There are opportunities big and small to take the ethical fork in the road:

- Passing off someone else's ideas or accomplishments as your own.
- Working at "half-mast" rather than putting in a productive day's work.
- Making personal long-distance calls and charging them to the company.
- Padding a travel expense report.
- Lying to customers and colleagues to cover for your mistakes rather than admitting them.
- Withholding payment to suppliers and using them for a free credit line.
- Paying kickbacks for business and referrals.
- Producing products or providing services of shoddy quality.
- Entering someone's computer or desk without authorization.
- Overbilling on by-the-hour projects.
- "Borrowing" from the petty-cash fund and failing to repay the money.
- Taking an employer's trade secrets or inside information and passing them to a new employer or to a competitor.
- Advertising deceptively or selling products known to be defective.
- Misrepresenting policy to employees and customers to avoid doing what you don't want to do.
- Giving undeserved, poor job references on employees to prospective employers.
- Repeating unverified, erroneous information or gossip, or failing to correct hurtful information that you hear passed on about someone or some situation.

Winning or losing, bounty or bankruptcy is not the point. Doing the right thing is.

● Padding a resume.

● Accepting a job and extensive training when you intend to stay with the job only until something else comes along.

● Failing to honor verbal commitments.

The particulars get sticky, at least to the person facing a complex situation and adverse conditions. That's why it's important to be firm and up front in our conviction always to do the ethical thing — BEFORE we discover the details of any adverse effects because of that choice. Why? In the heat of the situation, we tend to rationalize the "right" choice away.

Successful entrepreneur Vicky Weinberg talks about the choices she has to make as a developer of exclusive shopping malls and upscale subdivisions: "When you sign on a loan, you kind of throw your life away. Some of them pay out immediately, and on some of them, you're under the gun for a long time. Things are kind of scary when you sign a million-and-a-half dollar loan, and you have to have faith that the numbers the engineer gave you are correct — that you estimated everything properly. You've broken down all your costs, and you've tried to build in a survival kit if you have to hold your watch for two or three years, because all of a sudden there's a recession. I've learned that people move in and invariably homeowners are upset with this or that, a burned out light bulb or a hole in the pavement. But my word is my integrity in business. If there's a problem to be addressed, let me address it. When I tell people I'm going to do something, you can depend on me to do something."

In some cases, there's nobody who holds Vicky's feet to the fire when it comes to standing firm on her visions and plans. She may envision an esplanade one place and a canal at another. But when lots sell or don't sell, the revenue picture may take a turn for the worse during development. She has to keep in mind her commitment to the first people who purchased property in her development, about what she has described and committed to them in the way of amenities to the region. Developers, if they intend to stay in one part of the country, hold the "keys to the kingdom" in their hands when it comes to resale value for their property holders. Sometimes the specifics are in writing; sometimes they are not. In both cases, Vicky's bond is her word. Her future business depends on it. More importantly to her, her integrity demands it.

On the other hand, even in situations of the smallest financial risk, foolish women make foolish choices. Laurie, a small-time entrepreneur, runs a graphic design business out of her home office. She responded to an ad in the newspaper for a corporate client wanting some graphic design work done on technical manuals and some general word-processing done in transcribing cassette tapes.

They met briefly to discuss general capabilities and review Laurie's portfolio of work done for other clients. Then they discussed future projects and agreed to hourly rates. Laurie and the client began their relationship with the tape transcriptions as the first project, with a firm deadline of February 17. Laurie left her client's office with the tapes in hand and a promise to deliver them the following week.

On Monday, February 17, she phoned with this explanation: "I'm sorry to say I'm going to miss our very first deadline. I had a death in the family on Friday. My uncle passed away and I had to leave town for the weekend to attend the funeral. But I have completed all but seven of the tapes, and can deliver all of them by tomorrow at 2:00 p.m. Will that be acceptable?"

"Well, I'm sorry to hear about the death," the client responded. "But we do need them completed desperately. We're at a standstill on the project until we receive the transcriptions. I tell you what, I'll rearrange some things so as to keep everybody here working, and we'll see you tomorrow at 2:00."

The next morning at 11:00, Laurie phones the client. "I'm afraid I have some bad news. I was out of town overnight and returned to my home just a few minutes ago to discover that burglars hit last night. Just wiped us out. Everything. All of my office equipment — computers, printer. But I have your tapes. They didn't take the tapes."

"Well, that's good. I guess that was quite a shock."

"It's terrible. In fact, the police are here now, and we still

> *Vicky's bond is her word. Her future business depends on it.*

don't have a complete list of what else they've taken out of the house. It's a nightmare. It had to be somebody watching the house. I'm never gone overnight."

"Can you bring us the transcriptions you've done?"

"Well, I only have 22 printed out. And I don't have the disk. The disk was in the computer, and they stole that computer. I had started to print them out on Friday when I got the call about my uncle. I ran out of paper, and I intended to get more and finish printing them out over the weekend."

"Oh."

"But there's an upside in all this. I had already ordered a new computer — we were going to network them all together. It's supposed to arrive in the morning. I can use that to finish up, but I can't get them all to you until Friday, the 22nd."

"I hate to hear about the burglary, but I really need those tapes. Our entire project is at a standstill without those transcriptions."

"I understand. And I'm so sorry. I just can't apologize enough. I do want your business — the other projects — and I'm not even going to charge you the full fee on the ones I've done because of this delay."

"All right. We'll discuss that later. We'll see you on Friday."

On Thursday, the client called to ask what time Laurie would be delivering the tapes on Friday and reached only a voice-mail response. No return call.

On Friday, the client phoned again, leaving a second voice-mail and a page about the urgency of getting the tapes back, finished or unfinished. No return call. Finally, the client grew more suspicious and did some checking. The sheriff's department indeed had a burglary reported at the address given by Laurie — the previous June. Three more messages left on Laurie's voice-mail over the weekend produced no further response.

On Monday morning, the client phoned Laurie's pager number and left the number of a back-line at the office — one that Laurie wouldn't recognize. Sure enough, Laurie promptly returned that call. When Laurie discovered whose call she had returned, she again apologized profusely, "I'm terribly sorry for missing the deadline. The explanation would be just too bizarre, so I'm not even going to give it. I'll send the tapes and transcriptions completed by courier this morning." An hour later the incomplete project — only 14 transcriptions — arrived.

With the package was another letter of apology and a request that the client call her again on their next graphics or transcription project.

Unbelievable? No, not really. Probably if we talked to Laurie she would tell us that she intended to get the project done by the deadline, but underestimated her time. Instead of calling the client and telling the truth, she concocted one story and then another to buy more time. She probably never intended to "mess up the project." She simply responded to the situation according to her character, and her character dictated: Lie, when necessary, to save face or to save a deal.

Character dictates words, actions, decisions.

When caught in a tough place — with important or insignificant ramifications — we all act according to our internally programmed character. Character dictates words, actions, decisions.

I talk with people occasionally who argue the point. They say something to this effect: "Sure, I lie (or whatever) from time to time. But not about important stuff. I'd never lie or steal or misrepresent things in anything important."

I couldn't disagree more. Think of it this way: If Susan feels just a *little* pressure and decides to lie to downplay her part in the minor mishap to avoid a *little* embarrassment or inconvenience, think what she would do in a really tough situation to avoid *a lot* of pain — say, loss of a job, loss of a relationship, or loss of money. If people behave unethically in small situations, the pressure to do so in major situations will be even greater. Again, character controls.

After speaking at a convention, I was seated at the dinner table by an importer-exporter, and we discussed the topic of dealing with foreign companies. He assured me that the problem of unethical behavior in his export business in foreign countries was no less epidemic than in the US: "I've got a situation just now in Miami with a major airline. I'm going to write a letter Monday morning to the president of the airline and tell him we're no longer doing business with him."

I wanted to know why.

"Because they just laid off the last employee in Miami who I could depend on to tell me the truth about whether my shipment is going to get on the plane. You take it to the airline, and you know it has to get out immediately. The client in Latin America is waiting on it, and the airline will tell you it'll go out — when they know full well it won't.

"But I had this one guy — this *one guy* — who would always give me a truthful answer. He'd say, 'Norm, the shipment's not gonna get on that plane tonight.' In those situations, at least I could get on the phone and call my client on the other end and let them know.

"But the airline just did a major reorganization and they're laying people off. This guy's one of those who got axed. I'm hiring him. I'm making a place for him. Honest people are the kind I need. And I'm going to write the CEO of the airline and tell him why they're no longer getting my export business."

Smart women entertain only ethical options.

There is great personal power in being known as a person of character. Unlike circumstances, character always falls within our own control. It has nothing to do with beauty, bankruptcy, or bonds. It has everything to do with passion, persuasion, and power. Long-term success in business or personal relationships comes from being known as a woman of character, conviction, and commitment.

Smart women entertain only ethical options. To paraphrase Rick Warren in his *FAX of Life,* smart women consider their self-worth more important than their net worth.

7
Relish Relationships

S uccessful women — women who are successful in a worldly sense — often face failure with relationships. Many times they have relationships *in spite of* their success, not because of it. Both single and married women repeatedly find that many men are threatened by a woman's success. Because a primary drive in men is to be respected, men seek women who admire them, need them, and appreciate them.

Translated by many men, "appreciated" means men need women who will look to them for financial security and take the time either to contribute to their career effort or at least celebrate the recognition that comes their way from that effort.

Successful women have a different definition. Many married women spend an enormous amount of effort and time convincing their husbands they fulfill *emotional* needs inside them. The fact that women need men emotionally, and not because of their paycheck, should be a comfort to men. In many cases, it is not. Women fear that their success will destroy their marriage. It often does.

Successful women fear failure in relationships with their parents and kids as well. Mothers frequently choose to work their success around the lives of their children. They opt to sit in the auditorium and applaud at a school play rather than take the stage at a sales recognition meeting. As daughters, successful women may work their sales territory around the needs of an elderly parent.

As friends, successful women watch coworkers they are bypassing along the way and fear that the latest promotion or success may create jealousy that will damage the friendship. It's not an unfounded fear. Women care about relationships. They want to be liked and loved.

Smart women hold on to relationships, despite these fears, despite their success, and despite any difficulties. They don't NEED relationships literally, but they need them emotionally. That is, they don't feel inadequate and incomplete without them, but they thrive when relationships are in full bloom. Smart women fight for the time to cultivate and grow them.

Smart women hold on to relationships, despite these fears, despite their success, and despite any difficulties.

Put Family First

When it comes to marriage, smart women set up a partnership, not a holding company. That is, smart women and their spouses experience the satisfaction of going through life as partners, each giving to meet the needs of the other and, in return, having their own needs met. Marriages that operate like a holding company — with one of the partners holding all the sticks and doling out decisions by decree — wither.

Frequent national surveys of executive men report that these men often attribute their success to supportive wives. These men confirm that their wives have handled the household, family, and herself in such a way as to support, encourage, and enhance his opportunities for advancement. Likewise, married women who have chosen to devote time to a career appreciate husbands who support and encourage. Many of the executive women interviewed insist that their husbands provide just the emotional support they need to balance all their roles in life.

When it comes to marriage, smart women set up a partnership, not a holding company.

I have one of those supportive husbands. Is he weak himself? Hardly. He has faced the enemy in Vietnam. He has led a FEMA (Federal Emergency Management Agency) joint-service team in responding to national disasters. He has thrown himself between me and attacking dogs. He has delivered me safely to speaking audiences across several continents. Because he is competent and confident himself, he can be free to celebrate my successes.

When good things happen to me, my husband is the first to hang balloons in the office, order the cake, call the relatives, and buy me gifts. In fact, he is the best PR agent and cheerleader a wife could have. As best friends, I've come to trust his judgment implicitly. Because he enthusiastically supports my wins, I can hear him and trust him to tell me when I mess up. He's my closest confidante. He gives me emotional strength.

Here's what other women have to say about their partnerships with their husbands:

"My husband has helped me on everything from where to get a good haircut to doing spreadsheets with me at 3:00 a.m. And he encourages me in my other friendships. He laughs about my best friend, Colleen. He says to me, 'You could call her up and tell her you've just murdered someone, and she would say, 'Well, you probably had really good reasons.' He's just so supportive about everything."

Another: "My husband is a wonderful listener. When he and I do not have time to talk so that I can debrief my day or get his thinking, I feel totally stressed out — there's a clear meter there of how much time we've had based on my stress level."

Another: "Phil is a real support to me — a real positive that I didn't have in my prior relationship. He supports what I do and there's a high level of respect for my job and my contribution to it. He seems to take great pride in my doing well. That's significantly important to me."

Another: "Doug is my best friend. He is *always* available to me. And I know that I am his priority. I just know that he will always choose me."

One executive talks about the support her husband provided in the aftermath of a freak accident. She was trying to repair a toy for her toddler when it slipped out of her hand and struck him in the eye. As a result, her son had to have a cornea transplant and is legally blind. "It was not intentional, of course. Your mind knows that. But it is hard to stay focused on the fact that it was just a freak accident. You're faced with trying to patch one eye and force him to use the other eye. It was very traumatic. But my husband never for one split second pointed a finger or said anything that was hurtful or harmful. I had this terrible underlying guilt — it was absolutely the worst experience of my life — but he kept saying, 'Let's just focus on the future.' He's helped me deal with that."

Another executive tells about the team effort in raising their two teenage boys: "One of the most tumultuous times in my life was when our kids were teenagers. I was wanting Doug to step in and create this discipline for these kids and provide them more structure. I spent a lot of time in dialogue with our sons, trying to sort all that out. But now that they're young adults, I can see that Doug's way was the better way. He allowed them more freedom to make decisions — freedom that was good, that taught them to make good decisions for themselves."

Smart women know that the men and children in their lives provide great strength and support.

Parenting is easier and better as a partnership.

Smart women know that the men and children in their lives provide great strength and support. The extended family of parents, in-laws, and brothers and sisters also occupies a priority spot with smart women. Even across the miles, smart women make an effort to hold on to the extended family relationships that make life complete and give them a sense of well-being. They have come to understand the importance of having family "there," no matter what.

Families make the holidays a holiday. My own family, sixteen of us with parents and my brother and sister and their families, grab every opportunity we can find to spend time together. Whether that time involves eating too much good food, deciding on drapery colors, landscaping the yard, working on someone's resume, gathering the fallen pecans from the backyard, paddling a canoe, or sitting at the hospital during someone's surgery, I am fortunate.

Family provides the foundation for faith in the future.

Forgive and Forge On

Many people still deal with resentments and past hurts from parents, brothers and sisters, or grown children. We women apologize often, but we don't forgive nearly as easy. But smart women have spent time analyzing the difficult situation, gaining insight on motivations, and then decide to forgive. Forgiveness is a decision, always.

One interviewee tells about a rift between her sister, herself, and the rest of the extended family. "I had a sister whose morals were not what people expected back in the sixties. She had my parents paying for her 'education' when she wasn't even going to school. She had a baby before she married. She did a lot of things that hurt my parents. But just recently we had a 25-year anniversary party for her and her husband. I felt like everybody was trying to heal that wound that had been there for 25 years. At first I didn't feel that I should have to help fund an event like that to heal a wound. But evidently, that did it for her — she felt forgiven and accepted again by the family. I don't feel resentment anymore."

Forgiveness has limits for some people. For others, forgiveness flows from a deep well inside them. One interviewee tells about an unfaithful and alcoholic husband who, in the past, had created an enormous amount of pain for her and their children. Their years together were marred by his affairs and jail time on several occasions for hot checks, fights, and reckless driving due to the drinking. Here's how she explains her ability to forgive:

"It's important to me in relationships with people that if I say I'm going to do something, I want them to depend on me to do that. I intend to keep my word or my vow, no matter what. I promised God as a child that I would keep myself holy — not drink and not have sex before marriage, and those kinds of things. And I broke my promise as a teenager.

"Much later with Stu during the time he was so bad with the alcohol and the arrests, I really came to understand that verse in the Bible about forgiveness. It was totally out of context, but I was searching one night for meaning in all this.

Forgiveness is a decision, always.

I had no money or real talent to give to God, but I was searching for meaning in that verse about 'to whom much is given much is required.' At that moment, I was reminded of the forgiveness I'd been given and it reminded me to give forgiveness. It was a real turning point for me." As a footnote to her story, her husband has been sober now for several years and she does not regret her decision to forgive him.

Forgiveness from such deep wounds never comes easy. But time helps, and so does the experience of receiving forgiveness from others for our own mistakes and faults. As someone has already observed, we judge other people on their actions and results; but we want them to judge us on our intentions. Time and understanding give perspective on past hurts.

This woman's story reminds us of how much more forgiving we need to be on the relatively minor issues of family life. One woman with grown children and grandchildren summed up her realization this way: "When I lost my dad, I realized how important things like those little squabbles are. Having children myself, I now understand. No matter how hard you try to do what you think is really best for your kids, sometimes they misconstrue those things and they have their own little resentments of you. You think, *By golly, now I know how my own mom felt!* I didn't know I was making mistakes, but through things that have been called to my attention through our children, I have realized my mother was doing the very best she could."

Time and understanding give perspective on past hurts.

Hearing this woman reflect made me recall a similar realization in my own life several years ago when my children were in elementary school. On that occasion, I sat down and wrote my own parents a note. I share it with you now in the hopes that it triggers a similar realization for you. (My seventy-two-year-old mom, of course, has saved it all these years!)

Dear Mother and Daddy,

Two things recently have been on my mind the last couple of days, and they reminded me that I haven't written an "I love you" letter in a long time.

Yesterday when I had so many other things to do, I had to take time out and go to a "meeting of the mothers" and find out how to make Lisa's cheerleading costume and then spend hours sewing. She was excited and thrilled and eager to put it on and show it to the neighborhood kids — but not grateful enough to want to help around the house afterwards.

Of course, I realize that's part of being a child — near-sighted and selfish. But it reminded me again of all the times you sewed for me (when you hated it) and went to "mother meetings" when you were too busy. I was ungrateful then too, I'm sure. But now more and more, I see and love you for giving anyway despite my ingratitude as a child.

And then, Daddy, my taking Jeff to the doctor yesterday and paying $95 to put his knee in a brace and then knowing he shouldn't play football on it and listening to his griping about the brace and what he can't go outside to do because "we made him" keep the brace on. All that reminds me, Daddy, of the many times you spent money on our medical bills when you really couldn't afford it. How many times you let me play a basketball game with a cold or earache or sore throat, knowing it would probably mean another doctor bill and another prescription.

That's love we didn't evaluate much as kids. But I do now. I just wanted to say again, "I love you."

Dianna

Smart women cherish their family relationships.

No matter the size of your paycheck or the thrill of your industry's recognition, the loudest applause you will hear will be that of your family. Smart women cherish their family relationships.

Find Friends Who Offer an Emotional Support System

The question is not *if*; the question is *when*. If you have not experienced tragedies and crises in your life, you are a lucky person indeed. But you will. And when that time comes — the time when you have no family nearby and/or they are unwilling to come to your side — you will need friends. They are God's hands on earth. All but six of the women surveyed said they had a strong support system of friends.

In my gift book on friendship, *Fresh-Cut Flowers for a Friend,* I have tried to explore through my essays the value of friendships. For example:

*Sharing the happy-nings
in my life with you
has doubled my pleasure.
The same is true for the
disappointments — you've
made the doldrums
more bearable.*

*Thank you for stretching me.
For helping me to see
new ways of relating,
new causes to consider,
new interests to explore.*

*Thank you for saying things
to me that have not always
been easy to say. You risk my
hurt, disappointment, and
anger. But you say them
anyway. I appreciate that.*

> Many people now pay a therapist for what a friend used to do — listen.

Many people now pay a therapist for what a friend used to do — listen. Friends beat therapists in two ways: They don't make you sit on the couch, and they're far cheaper!

We don't need to look far to understand the value of friendship. In his book, *Emotional Intelligence,* David Goleman points out some amazing research about the value of emotional support. He writes: "Perhaps the most powerful demonstration of the clinical power of emotional support was in groups at Stanford University Medical School for women with advanced metastatic breast cancer. After an initial treatment, often including surgery, these women's cancer had returned and was spreading through their bodies. It was only a matter of time, clinically speaking, until the spreading cancer killed them. Dr. David Spiegel, who conducted the study, was himself stunned by the findings, as was the medical community: women with advanced breast cancer who went to weekly meetings with others survived *twice as long* as did women with the same disease who faced it on their own."

The same is true for men.

Goleman continues about similar studies showing the importance of emotional ties to men: "Perhaps the most telling testimony to the healing potency of emotional ties is a Swedish study published in 1993. All the men living in the city of Goteborg who were born in 1933 were offered a free medical exam; seven years later the 752 men who had come for the exam were contacted again. Of these, 41 had died in the intervening years. Men who had originally reported being under intense emotional stress had a death rate three times greater than those who said their lives were calm and placid.... Yet among men who said they had a dependable web of intimacy — a wife, close friends, and the like — there was no relationship whatever between high stress levels and death rate. Having people to turn to and talk with, people who could offer solace, help, and suggestions, protected them from the deadly impact of life's rigors and trauma."

What makes up a family or support system? Yours includes those people who give you unconditional love, make you feel that you belong, recognize your achievements, help you in crises, and encourage you in difficulties. A support system may be people who depend on each other, participate in a common activity, make decisions together, and commit themselves for the long-term or short-term to each other's well-being. In other words, community is a state of "being." To develop this support system around you:

Be interested.

Be interesting.

Cry with them.

Be happy when they win.

Do favors for them.

Let them do favors for you.

I heard a wonderful way to categorize friends not long ago while watching *Good Morning America.* I didn't catch the name of the guest or I would give her credit here for the original wording, but paraphrased here is her description of the various stages of friendship that psychologists have been trying to capture in their writing for years: You make a connection on some commonality. Then you and the other person *hang out together* (your relationship moves out of context, such as work, and you go out for pizza together). You can measure the next stage of friendship by those who are willing to *hang in with you* during the tough times. Finally, the deepest stage of friendship is when friends *hang on with you* across the miles and through the years. Those that hang out, hang in, and hang on — these are your most valuable friendships.

Those that hang out, hang in, and hang on — these are your most valuable friendships

Let me share three special times with friends in my own life — times that illustrate the mind-set, behavior, and sacrifice of friends. One from a longtime friend in my life: I had difficulties in my second pregnancy and had to stay in bed for five months before my second child was born. My friend, with four small children of her own, came to see me almost every day of that five-month period. Sometimes she brought only a smile, at other times a library book or a casserole, and one time a complete notebook of quotes and Bible verses on friendship all hand copied.

This is friendship.

The second longtime friend and I walked together every evening for almost a year while she and I both searched our souls for direction in life after a failed and failing marriage. We cried over the pain of unfaithfulness, laughed about unrealistic expectations of 19-year-old brides, complained about selfish teens trying our limits, prayed about being able to go to work on a difficult day, shared cherished promises from God, tried to sort out lessons learned, and worked on opening each other's blind spots.

This is friendship.

A third, new friend congratulated me when I won and she

lost. Although neither of us at the time knew it, the producers at *Good Morning America* contacted both of us authors to appear as experts on the same subject for the same feature slot. When I phoned to tell her the news that my book had been selected, she told me about being contacted also. Her response? To send a fax to the show's producers telling them that they'd made a wise choice!

This is friendship.

An entrepreneur talks about having her friend around when several tragedies happened all at once: "My friend calls me 'queen of de'nial.' My business was stressful, a significant relationship had just broken up. My mom had been sick for years and had died two years earlier with cancer, and I had other serious illnesses in the family. Then I had one of those identity crises. Who am I? What do I do next? What have I been spending my time on? I was in this frantic mood, where everything is glittery and wonderful, kind of like the party before the funeral. And then it just all came to a halt. I lost it, but she knew just what to say and what to do. I had to let out a lot of stuff while I was with this friend. There wasn't any fear. There wasn't any risk. Just being with this person."

This is friendship.

From a single woman: "I was in the hospital in ICU for five days when it was touch and go. It was very important to me that people knew about it and were praying. And then I went through this really scary time with my job, not knowing if I'd have one or not. I drew on friends heavily just to verbalize about losing my job over this. I needed to hear a friend acknowledge, 'You almost died.'"

From a mother of a teen: "In a situation with my son, he was getting willfully disobedient and I was getting increasingly angry. I was very close to slapping him, and I've never done that before. It frightened me that the whole thing was to that point. I just left and went to my friend's office — right in the middle of the day."

This is friendship.

Another: "When word got around that I lost the big opportunity I was so excited about, my friends in the professional community came to the rescue and started offering me work, which really did help me to start believing in myself again."

Another: "Well, last February, my son called up and said his best friend had killed himself. When I was talking to him about it, he told me that he'd had the same thoughts. He'd had some disappointments, and he just needed to get away, to get some counseling, and to get into another job. I called up Rebecca, and boom, she said, 'Send him. I'll get him a job!' And she did. That probably saved his life."

This is friendship.

Another: "My sixteen-year-old son had a bad, bad accident. I was out of the office for three months, and at the time I managed a group of over 1,000 people. Every night they provided dinner for me and my family. For three months. Every night."

This is friendship.

"Presence is

as important

as words."

Another single woman: "I had this massive project that I was doing over the past weekend, just real drudge work. I was prepared to make it an all-nighter. Well, about 7:30 I had a couple of friends breeze by and ask me to go out to dinner and a movie. I told them I couldn't — that I had this project to get done. Without any further explanation, they started taking off their coats, putting down their pocketbooks, taking off their scarves, and saying, "Great, hand us the work." They stayed all night — until 6:30 the next morning. It was something I would have never *asked* anybody to do."

This is friendship.

As one director of nursing puts it to her nursing staff: "Presence is as important as words." Time does not matter. When does friendship happen? A conversation here. A conversation there. A feeling shared. A deed done. A favor requested. A soul bared. You wake up one day and have a valued friend.

Communicate With Colleagues

Although certainly not as vital as family and friends, colleagues also come in handy along the way. You basically need two kinds of coworkers: Those who can provide expertise or information you need through informal networking channels and those you can communicate with on a trust level. You trust them to shoot straight with you and see your needs as a person.

For those who can provide information and expertise, smart women network. They find a mentor and become a mentor. For those women who say they can't find anyone who will give them the time they need to learn and grow, I always ask, "Who have you taken under your wing and mentored along?" The old saying, "What goes around comes around," is an old saying because it's true. Its triteness doesn't invalidate its truth. You give help to get help. Word travels. People observe.

Many of the smart women I interviewed spoke highly of various women's networks and professional associations. Away from their closest colleagues, sharing with other executive and professional women gave smart women a chance to bounce ideas off each other, seek advice on problems and issues, and gain support as women. Some are formal, like the Mary Kay director's weekly "success meetings," where the women gather to share their sales successes and earn pats on the back from each other.

Other networks are more informal, put together by anyone who takes the lead in finding other people with similar interests and situations. For some informal groups, the more dissimilar the women involved, the better. One particular president of her own company says they have a group of four women who meet over breakfast once a month to share what's happening in their lives.

In fact, one executive of the group received an immediate payoff of the time invested when she was leaving her corporate position. The company had offered her a severance package that she felt was adequate and was about to accept when she called one of the four colleagues to talk things over. That friend rushed right over, put pencil to paper with her, and showed her that the severance package wasn't nearly what it should be for her tenure and contribution. The resigning

Away from their closest colleagues, sharing with other executive and professional women gave smart women a chance to bounce ideas off each other, seek advice on problems and issues, and gain support as women.

woman was able to double her severance package after their discussion. In other words, these professional associations served the same kind of functional role as boards of directors have played for corporate CEOs for years.

But we're not just talking dollars. We're talking sense. Several women tell of annual "retreats" they take with friends, with nothing heavier than shopping and children's holiday parties on their minds. One such woman and eleven former college roommates meet every other year for a long weekend to catch up on each other's lives and to lighten the load of life by dividing it among twelve. Another woman has organized a weekend shopping spree to a resort town with eight other friends from all walks of life. They rent a van, pile in, and talk nonstop for 48 hours.

What do such formal and informal networks do for you? Those who participate say these get-togethers provide perspective on their own situation as they compare it to others' family life. They gain support for handling tough times, like a delinquent son, a cancer diagnosis, a crumbling marriage, a stress-producing boss, or a mother with Alzheimer's. In other words, they've built enough trust during these short retreats that they feel free to call on each other for other "events" or situations during the intervening weeks or months.

Keep confidences.

To grow these relationships with colleagues, first develop and express mutual respect for their work. Then be discerning about what you ask and tell them; be careful not to put them in the tight spot of having to refuse to share confidential information. Finally, let them know you're human — speak up when you need their help and offer them yours.

Show People You Need Them

How do you go about building those kinds of relationships? Find things in common. Invite them to meet you for an activity outside work or your formal association. Be transparent. Reveal your heart to them. Listen — even when you're not in the mood. Don't pass judgment on what they say or do. Keep confidences. Find something you can do for them. All these steps in building friendships, we know, we've experienced.

But this last step — letting people know you need them — some women find difficult. We women have trouble speaking up sometimes. It's hard to say things like, "My daughter is giving me problems; can you tell me how you've handled x? Or: "My mom has to have someone help her with her therapy exercises next Thursday, and I have to be gone for three days. Do you know of someone who could come by?" We have to get over our reluctance to call for help when life is overwhelming. People are so busy today with their own lives that they literally do not take the time to notice when others have special needs — or they hear about the need three weeks too late.

Sometimes successful women feel reluctant to call for help because others haven't called on them. Those with slimmer paychecks may look at the more successful women and assume that their money can buy whatever services they need. That may be true, but that's not the point. Again, it's not always the physical assistance but the emotional support that becomes most valuable in times of crises.

Smart women ask others for what they need, not in a burdensome way and not repeatedly so that they take advantage of others. But they do ask.

Smart women ask others for what they need...

People need to be needed. They need to feel magnanimous. They need to feel generous with their time and their resources and their emotional strength. A request for help is often interpreted as: "Thank you for seeing that magnanimous spirit inside me. Thank you for considering me a generous, caring person. Thank you for considering our relationship close enough to ask."

Some women make the mistake of presenting themselves to the world as someone who needs no one. Though we as women may have had to do that years ago to prove to those in the boardroom that we were "tough enough," women need relationships. If you're one of those women who "hangs back," not wanting to trouble others when you need them, step forward. Others want to "hang in" with you. If you're fortunate, they'll "hang on" with you through the years.

Sometimes the quickest way to find a friend is to show that you need one.

Don't Depend on Others To Make You Happy

Having said all this about relationships, relationships work only when you don't need them to stay mentally healthy and whole. The situation is much like going to the bank for a loan: You have to show them you don't need the money before they'll give it to you.

If you look for relationships because you're a needy person, you throw things off balance. That doesn't mean you don't need relationships. Instead, it means that you can't approach the relationship with your cup out — waiting on a spouse, a child, a parent, a colleague, or a friend to fill it up time and time again. You approach the relationship with your cup full and look for opportunity to pour half into theirs when it's empty.

Those smart women who live alone do relish their relationships with extended family and friends, but they have also learned to enjoy solitude.

You cannot approach any other human being and say — aloud or with actions — make me happy. That burden is much too much to bear for another person, no matter how much they love you. Each of us is responsible for our own happiness.

How do you find happiness within yourself? How does your cup become full? The ten smart moves I am offering you in this book are essential to finding happiness within yourself. And when you integrate them into your life, you'll find that you are less dependent upon others for your sense of well-being and you have a healthy friendship to offer others.

Learn To Enjoy Solitude as Punctuation Between People

So where does that leave single women without a spouse or children? Not necessarily lonely. There's a great deal of difference between being alone and being lonely. Those smart women who live alone do relish their relationships with extended family and friends, but they have also learned to enjoy solitude. Many women who live alone are healthy and happy. Rather, it's the feeling of being cut off from others that makes women feel lonely.

Ask some traveling professional women why they order room service for dinner, and they will tell you that despite the extra cost, they'd prefer to eat in their room rather than enter a restaurant alone. Some women echo the same reason about why they don't like to go to a party, attend church, or enroll in a continuing education course alone. Some women even rush into a marriage despite misgivings because of the hidden motivator — fear. It is often more powerful than love. Some fear growing old alone. Some fear facing everyday life in the present.

Smart women have *learned* to be content within themselves. All but two women on the survey reported that they *enjoy* times of solitude. More than *enjoy* — most used the word *love* in connection to solitude. They fill their time with reading, gardening, crafts, exercising, listening to music, playing the piano, prayer, meditation, nature walks, sewing, rubber-stamping, driving, watching sunrise and sunset, sports, journal writing, cooking, surfing the Internet, walking in the cemetery, walking the dog, wandering in the library.

Smart women relish solitude in small doses along with their relationships.

Smart women cherish and cultivate their relationships. Those relationships with family, friends, and colleagues provide emotional support, intellectual stimulation, and physical help. When the career ends, family and friends remain. Smart women work hard to keep relationships in good repair.

Smart women have learned to be content within themselves.

8
Bend So You Don't Break

When tornadoes hit, things either bend or snap. I've lived through them and seen the aftermath. Straws blown through telephone polls. Two-by-fours stuck through trucks. Earrings embedded in cement.

Sometimes life's events strike with such force that those who don't bend snap. Bending in response to fears, disappointments, setbacks, conflicts, and tragedies keeps life from breaking you. To be sure, there are other ways to cope. Some people grow more rigid in their purposes, plans, and positions. They try to anesthetize themselves to the pain through drugs, alcohol, sleep, overeating, fighting, sex, or suicide.

A tiny voice inside them cries out, "You don't have what it takes." "You can't do that." "They have it in for you." "You ought to be ashamed." "Nobody expects you to do more/better." "God is punishing you; you deserve this." "You should just give up — it won't happen for you." "Don't tell anybody what you want, so they won't know when you fail." "Life isn't fair."

They become immobilized by their fear, their pain, their disappointment — in themselves, in others, in life.

But smart women know how to endure, survive, and even thrive despite adversity. They understand flexibility. Their fear flames into energy to alter their course and finish the race.

If we expect to stand in the difficult times, we have to

But smart women know how to endure, survive, and even thrive despite adversity.

stretch and build our flexibility in the small things of life. For example, our relationships with our children as they grow to become adults become a lesson in flexing between our role as parent and that of friend. As a mother, I have had to move from wrapping my daughter in a blanket for a nap to letting her tell me how to wrap her newborn for his nap.

As a business woman for the past eighteen years, I've had to stay flexible to survive the changes in our industry. When I first started the business, all I had to know how to do was teach business and technical writing courses to engineers. Then I had to learn to recruit and train new employees and manage a business. I had to learn to write proposals to win the big contracts. There was the matter of understanding accounting principles and financial ratios. Then the training delivery method changed from stand-up training in the classroom to self-directed learning through CD-ROM, satellites, and the Internet.

We have to bend to keep from breaking our spirit and our dreams.

Companies that can't be flexible won't be around for long. Remember what happened to behemoth IBM when people started moving away from mainframes to personal computers? Remember what happened to American auto makers when they refused to listen to people who wanted smaller, more fuel-efficient cars? Businesses bend to keep their bottom-line intact.

The same proves true with individuals. We have to bend to keep from breaking our spirit and our dreams.

Learn To Deal with Disappointment

Life deals us disappointments. Disappointments over marriages that fail. Disappointments about children who make wrong choices. Disappointments about careers that don't unfold as we have been promised. Disappointments about friends who desert us and family who ignore us. Disappointments unfold often when we least expect them.

How often have we read past those lines in contracts that say "nothing but a violent act of God" and given them little thought? Jeannine Brannon, in the process of changing her career, thought she had signed an ironclad contract with an insurance company as their representative in the Fort Lauderdale, Florida, area. For a year, she worked to become certified, taking all the tests and attending seminar after seminar to learn the business. With her husband between jobs and two small children dependent on her, she signed her employment contract two weeks before Hurricane Andrew hit the Florida coast.

That "violent act of God" clause in the contract was just what the insurance company needed to void her employment contract and restructure the entire insurance region. Because Fort Lauderdale was a high-risk area, the company decided not to replace their agents in that area. For the first time in her life, Jeannine found herself in the middle of a career disappointment she could not alter or control. With nothing to "fix," she had no decision left but to move on with life.

Aside from career disappointments, another common disappointment and challenge for many women has been the flexibility of bending their dreams, plans, and family life around a husband's career.

Cynthia Latham talks about her marriage to a chemical engineer, employed by a large oil company. For their entire married life, his assignments have taken him from plant to plant, from city to city. She explains, "I feel like my life is on a back burner in a way. Sometimes I like to plan things, like going back to graduate school. But if I can't complete the program within a matter of months, I have to wait. I just say, 'Well, I don't have the time to get into it — I know I'll be gone before I can finish it. Why bother?'"

Debbie Henderson has moved about every three years because of her husband's career — so often that she could not establish herself in the career she wanted early on. But with her teaching credentials, she was always able to find a teaching job wherever they landed. In one particular situation, she spent one year just getting into the educational environment. She spent her second year substantiating the need for a deaf-education program in the community. Then in the third year, she finally received funding for the program. Once the program was in place, she won several commendations from the community for the effort. She built relationships with the hospital community and the PTA to get educational and audiology services for her kids. She then began work counseling the parents of her hearing-impaired students about their kids' needs. Just when things were up and running, her husband got transferred again. She had to walk away from it all.

Wives understand disappointments, discouragements, and derailment of plans. And when you become a mother, parenting once again changes things. If not the actual substance of our goals, your children alter the path to reach them. That path becomes circuitous.

Jane Handly remembers the momentum she had built after having made her successful movie. She had just finished her master's degree and was working in community colleges to instruct teachers how to put arts into the basic school curriculum. Then her husband lost his job and their entire situation became very unstable. With a child still in kindergarten, she needed a more stable home environment and income. So Jane moved back into the classroom for ten more years until she could once again pick up the path to her personal dreams on the stage.

These smart women love their children and cherish them as gifts. Nevertheless, parenting demands flexibility.

These smart women love their children and cherish them as gifts. Nevertheless, parenting demands flexibility. Ask any mother who has gotten herself dressed in the morning before the baby spits up.

The pain of *not* having children can be one of life's biggest disappointments. Sue Morris tells about the period in her life when she and her husband wanted a child so badly — before, she says, God answered her prayer through adoption. Why do we become so disappointed? As Sue puts it, "You grow up with certain expectations about how life should be and ours just wasn't that way."

Another woman of expectations has experienced the helpless feeling of infertility. "I have always been a goal-driven, achievement-oriented person. I always felt that if I wanted something badly enough — if I just did the right things — I could get anything I wanted. Success will come to those who wait — that sort of thing. It was a real startling reality for me to finally accept the fact that there are some things you really can't control. A friend of mine said, 'There's a difference between a desire and a goal. You can have a really strong desire for something, but it really can't be your goal unless you can make it happen.' That's what I found out about infertility."

In almost any case, expectations lead to disappointment. About ourselves. About our marriages. About our careers. About our children. And disappointments can do us in — or deal us a better hand. Eventually, with perspective, disappointments in life develop in us an attitude of gratitude.

Bend, So Conflict Doesn't Break You

For some of us, conflicts with others at home and on the job demand the greatest flexibility. Several interviewees told about being placed in a situation with a boss, coworker, or subordinate who pushed their capacity to understand and cope to the limits.

One insightful woman theorized this way about her boss: "My boss seemed to be so aware of my weaknesses that he seemed to set me up to fail. He was not only quick to point out those weaknesses, but was also quick to deflate anything I achieved. I got into the trap of structuring a lot of what I did and establishing my own priorities around what I felt would prove him wrong in his assessment of me. I finally moved to a different area of responsibility so that my day-to-day life was not impacted by him. But it was years before I gained perspective on the situation."

Other interviewees talked about being forced to follow policy, though not unethical, that they thought harmful to others in their organization. Some have had to make hiring and firing decisions with which they did not agree. Some have had to leave their jobs because of conflict they faced with an executive team about how to handle certain processes, divisions, projects, or products.

Sometimes the conflict that disappoints involves personal relationships.

One thirty-six-year-old tells about her attempts to remake the man she loved but never married: "He was a doctor, a Vietnam vet, a classic Vietnam vet. He didn't talk. He had all these war wounds, and I'm not making light of it, because my brother was there too. But the doctor's personnae was just 'I don't talk. I am a real man, and nobody gets close to me. I have all these secrets, and I don't talk about them.' So my goal was: I will change him. I will get him to open up to me; he will do it for me. If I can be more loving, more interesting, more of everything, I can win him over and break him out of his shell. We will be the two people who live happily forever after. And that never, never happened. It just never happened. Whatever secrets he had are still his. I gave up. I was just sure I could change him. I could not."

There are legions of women who have traveled that same path — who have dated or married a man to remold and remake him. Love provides only so much flexibility. Either the love breaks or the person breaks. A heart that is rigid in love often breaks both people involved. Even love — or more especially love — demands elasticity.

Conflict, if we stiffen ourselves to it, can harden our resolve and mar our character. Or, if we let it, conflict can polish our skills and shine our temperament.

Bend So Anger and Hurt Don't Break You

Resentment makes you inflexible emotionally. You fix your thoughts on whoever or whatever has wronged you, and having your eye on that target, you can see no other.

One mother of three tells about the turmoil her family has been through with a troubled child. Tricia and her husband adopted two toddlers, and they became a happy family of four. Then soon after, she became pregnant and they became a nuclear family of five. But their family of five began to explode from the anger bottled inside their adopted three-year-old son.

As they moved around the country, their early years of family life were marked by counselor after counselor. Some were excellent, some were incompetent, who did a lot of damage to both mother and son. The son's preteen and early teen years were scarred by anger, defiance, running away, and acting out. Finally, out of desperation, after one occasion when Riley had run away from home, Tricia came to the end of her rope. "I cannot let you come home and tear our family apart again. It hurts us all too much." But he came home again. And left again. And again. And again.

With everyone in the family crying one evening, Tricia pleaded with Riley, "What *is it* you want? Just please, tell me, what is it you *want*?"

"I want to live somewhere else!" he yelled, with his anger pitted against the world.

Tricia and her husband decided to put Riley in a home for troubled youth, where they could provide for him financially but let professionals work with him on a daily basis. During the troubled times while away from home, he would call occasionally: "Hi, Dad, how are you? Could I talk to Mom?" But she was so hurt and so worn out that she couldn't talk to him for almost a year.

Forgiveness allows flexibility of the heart when the head says it can take no more.

During this time, Riley decided to get in touch with his birth mother. After letters back and forth, Riley realized that his birth mother did not lead a lifestyle that welcomed him. Tricia says she doesn't know exactly what happened inside her son at that point, but something inside him changed. He asked to come home one last time.

Her hurt faded; the forgiveness poured out. She accepted him back into their home. Since he's returned at age sixteen, he has rejoined his school organizations and made a name for himself on the debate team. Is it working out? Tricia sums up, "On all the weekend trips, I go along as sponsor. He wants me there. For the approval. Always, he asks me to be there."

Forgiveness allows flexibility of the heart when the head says it can take no more.

Bend So You Can Manage the Downside of Risks

Life is about taking calculated risks. Those that don't pan out play hard on our emotions. But smart women know that all risks don't work out as they had planned. If they did, they wouldn't be called risks.

Our flexible attitude — the rubber band around failures that helps us bounce back — makes the thought of risk-taking more acceptable.

Chris Casady took the biggest risk of her life when, after graduate school, she moved to New York City to make it as an actress. Sink or swim, that was her dream — to snag enough parts to make a decent living without having to wait tables as so many other artists have to do, waiting their turn for the BIG picture.

Chris understood the risk. From information put out by the Screen Actors Guild, she knew that females receive only 30 percent of the available roles, while males win 70 percent of the parts. Only 6 percent of all roles go to females over the age of 40. Was it a risk worth taking? According to Chris, yes, if you're flexible. As she approached that big 4-0, she began to see that her screen career was about to come to an end. Then, on the set one day while working in a program for Mead Johnson, a client planted in her mind the idea of becoming a corporate spokesperson.

That flexibility of thinking proved to be the beginning of her second career.

Another smart interviewee tells about marrying a widower with three teenage children: "I can remember saying to a friend, 'Well, it [the marriage] can't make much difference [in my lifestyle and responsibilities] because he has a full-time, live-in housekeeper.' I was so naive. It took me three years, four years maybe, to just get myself back on track after moving into a very complex family structure. My husband was a recovering alcoholic and I knew nothing about the alcoholic family structure. I came to know a lot. It's just such a different way of living than I had ever been personally exposed to." She adapted, and they have a wonderful marriage.

For others, managing the downside of risky decisions doesn't turn out so well.

Entrepreneur Judith Briles has been through much more than most people in withstanding the storms of life. She suffered at the hands of a physically abusive husband, and two of her children have died. Here is part of her later story in her own words: "One of the things I used to do in the old days was raise money to invest. I was in real estate and would buy old buildings to renovate and rent them back to a new life. The big downfall came when my partner, who was the contractor, embezzled money and got involved in drugs.

"It all disappeared. It was my personal signature on the $750,000 loan. We wiped out. It was a horrible, horrible disaster. In the middle of all that, I got ill. I had three surgeries in ten months. I got cancer. The business went under. My son died. It was a horrible time. Would I want to go back and do it all again? Are you kidding? But I do know that it threw me in another direction. There are yeses behind the nos, but you have to be open and receptive to receive them. If you're stuck on 'How come this happened to me?' or 'How come we're going through this or that?' or "If only I'd done this,' you'll never allow yourself to experience the other good things life has to offer."

Judith understands bouncing back. She understands flexibility.

So do other smart women. Consider the downside before you start the uphill climb. Can you live with the results if things don't pan out as you had hoped? Courage comes into play when you know the odds and you can bend your attitude to accommodate the fallout.

Bend To Survive Tragedy

Dora Grider, herself a victim of multiple sclerosis, has known disappointment. She knows about the frightening experience of willing your body to do something it won't. The first few symptoms of her disease appeared shortly after she had begun a food basket business. Her clients were corporations that ordered from 50 to 500 hams or turkeys for her to deliver to their employees on special occasions.

Her business plan sounded ideal for her young family. As a former employee of an ad agency, she knew that Houston had only one food basket business and needed another. When her boss at the ad agency began to pressure her to work longer hours, the food basket business became her game plan to control her own hours and life. For the first three years, she ran the business from her home. Then, because of its rapid growth, she decided to move to a commercial location. At about that time, the *Houston Business Journal* did a huge spread on her company.

The day the newspaper article hit, Dora was stricken with paralysis on her right side. Her job was hard physical work — work with her hands that she increasingly could no longer control. She got the word out to friends and family that she would need to find a buyer for her business.

Although Dora jokes with her husband that she's moving into her "high maintenance" years, she has learned to wrap her life and dreams — and a new mortgage-assistance business — around her illness.

Entrepreneur Vicky Weinberg has also experienced a tough few years early in life. She lost her father, whom she was very close to, had a difficult situation with her family business, and sat by her husband's side as he took chemotherapy to destroy his cancer. But she learned to bend under these blows. She loves the flexibility of her real-estate development business: "I could stay with Steve to help with his chemo. I could work out of my house. I have a computer that I go back and forth with. I have my voice mail that I've made part of my life since my son was born. He is my priority."

Kathy Harless, president of a large subsidiary of a Fortune 500 company, also learned how quickly life can be cut short when her fifteen-year-old son was involved in a terrible car accident three years ago. For months, he was at the point of death. He survived, but lost his sight in one eye. Her athletic son had played every sport his school offered, and just helping him adjust to the trauma took two long years.

She insists she has always had her family priorities in the right order, but her son's accident gave her an even stronger perspective about what is really important in the big scheme of things: "When people sit in the conference room and argue about things — things that are so minor — you have to laugh. Those things are not what life is about."

During the time she was away from work and basically cocooning with her husband and recuperating son, friends of the family had urged them to go out to dinner just to take a break from the situation. Once at the restaurant, the valet parked the car and they went inside to enjoy a quiet meal.

About halfway through the salad course, the maitre'd announced loudly, "Who drives a black LHS?"

Her husband looked up and answered, "That's ours."

"Then please follow me."

Once outside, her husband took in the situation. It seems that after the valet had parked the car, another patron's car had come flying over the hedges and landed on top of their LHS. He surveyed the situation and returned to the restaurant table to rejoin his wife and host.

Kathy asked, "Is there a problem?"

"No," he deadpanned. "They just double-parked our car."

After his explanation, they simply looked at each other. Kathy shrugged, "Oh, well, thank goodness we weren't in it." They finished dinner without interruption.

Attitude is paramount in assimilating the tragedies of life, sorting the significant from the trivial, and bouncing back when your heart is breaking.

Sometimes you find that you have to carry other people's tragedies along with your own. JoAnn Blackmon faced heartache when her husband's parents became dependent on her at the height of her sales career with Mary Kay. Her mother-in-law discovered she had cancer and her father-in-law was a wheelchair bound, double amputee. Both came to live with JoAnn for three years, during which time she had to put her career plans on hold.

Emotionally distraught, although not resentful that life had dealt her this turn, she leaned on her understanding of the corporate philosophy of Mary Kay: faith first, family second, and career third. Her CEO's philosophies led her to put her priorities in order during this difficult time. JoAnn had already been crowned Queen of Sales for her stellar performance and

Attitude is paramount in assimilating the tragedies of life, sorting the significant from the trivial, and bouncing back when your heart is breaking.

had nothing but more successes looming on the horizon. But three years after she had reigned as Mary Kay Sales Director, she had to start over. Today, she has regained her momentum and continues to travel the world (Hong Kong, Switzerland, Bermuda, Germany, Greece, France, Spain, Portugal) in her new found freedom.

Would she do it all again — make the same sacrifice to care for her in-laws? "Professionally, it cost me a lot, but that's not the most important thing in life. I feel I did the right thing."

Jane Handly reflects on her mother's fight with Alzheimer's. "Alzheimer's has been a study in helplessness. I've watched my daddy deal with it through alcoholism. It has deteriorated the core family, and you can't fix those things. You pray about it. You think about it. You read about it. You try to manipulate it. You can't fix it. You can't. It's just unbelievably hard."

Just because we label it tragedy doesn't mean a situation doesn't hammer our self-esteem. Those who have experienced tragedy often blame themselves, which adds to their pain.

Becky Noecker's mother had been put on drugs for an ulcer. Late one evening, Becky's brother called to tell her that he was worried about their mother's depression. Her sister called with the same concern. Then her dad got on the phone. Finally, Becky got all three of them on a conference call and had them put her mother on the phone with them while she attempted to assess the depth of her condition. "Mom, everybody is worried about how depressed you are, and they are even worried that you might commit suicide."

"Yes," was all she said.

That was all it took for Becky to put her in the hospital and go to stay at her side. They spent a week together while her mother was in the hospital. Her mother improved, and the doctor decided to discharge her the following day. Becky had two babies she had been ignoring for a week, so she left that evening. Her mother hung herself in the hospital the next morning before she was discharged.

How did Becky deal with the tragedy? "It was a huge depression for me. I felt it was my fault — that I should have known, that I could have done something. You have to deal with it. You have to educate yourself. I learned that depression was a side effect of the medicine. You have to educate yourself and recognize that it wasn't your fault. As successful women, we think everything is within our control. It isn't."

Few of us have such real lifelong, life-altering limitations placed on us. The thing that limits us more often, and most catastrophically, is our attitude about these limitations and tragedies: a defeatist outlook, self-doubt, self-pity, worry, lack of self-discipline, and lack of faith.

In our culture, we emphathize and sympathize with victims — but we don't respect them. We want heroes and heroines who inspire us as they fight against great odds. We admire the indomitable spirit of people who bounce back. We applaud people who study their options and take action. We want them to do the best they can with what they have where they are.

Smart women bend, rather than break, during life's difficulties.

But having said that, as I listen, live, and learn, I have come to this conclusion: In some tragedies, the only true choice we have is our reaction. The only thing we can do is pray. The only opportunity we have is growth. For smart women, these are enough. Smart women learn to bend their career, their goals, their will, and their heart so that hard times don't break their spirit. Smart women bend, rather than break, during life's difficulties.

9
Seek Spiritual Guidance

T
he roles of wife, mother, friend, and employee hold their shape best when women wear a spiritual foundation. So how does that idea fit with your spiritual understanding?

"Spiritual" has become a buzz word of late. According to a recent *Forbes* magazine article ("Bringing Religion to the Boardroom," April 7, 1997), there is a religious revival in the US. Bible study in the boardroom has become common and chic.

In various contexts, people have used the term *spiritual* to mean living a life based on some code of morality or ethics. For others, spirituality means doing good deeds in the world, serving humanity. For others, spirituality means worshipping nature and protecting the environment. To still others, it means commitment to political ideologies and responsibility to future generations.

Though all are worthwhile intentions and pursuits, these are very limiting visions of our spiritual nature and the spiritual dimension in our universe.

Simplify Your Life So You Have Time for a Spiritual Focus

The first step in gaining a broader spiritual view of the universe is to make time and space in your life to gaze out the window. How to find more time has haunted harried women for the past decade. With bar exams, promotions, soccer tryouts for the kids, and award banquets for husbands, how do you find extra time to take on yet another "opportunity" in life?

For most of us, our days are so full that we need to subtract something before we can add other things. If you are one of those people, here are some test questions that might help you determine priorities: Start by looking at your to-do list or your calendar. Stop on each item to ask:

● How much time does this routine or activity require in my life?

● How much money is this routine or activity costing me?

● Do I really need/want this routine or activity in my life?

● Is this issue, activity, or situation causing stress in my family relationships?

● Will this issue, activity, or situation be important to me two years from now? Five years from now? Ten years from now?

● What is the long-term payoff for my investment of emotional energy and time?

Do you see anything you can subtract? On the other hand, do you see anything that creates passion in your life, that lights up your spirit? It is generally not the boring routine that causes burnout, but the absence of passion and purpose.

Many well-known women have developed a passion about their purpose for living. They have devoted themselves to ideas, goals, and missions that will last well past their own years. For example, Mary Kay Ash has devoted time and millions of dollars to research on cancers primarily affecting women. Barbara Jordan used her stature and religious heritage, along with a huge intellect, to teach her university students about morality and ethics. Elizabeth Dole's work with the Red Cross has made the difference in so many lives during tragic circumstances. As a physician and university professor, Elizabeth Paeth Lasker has made the world a better place through taking very complex medical material — specifically, her work on nutrition — and putting it into terms

It is generally not the boring routine that causes burnout, but the absence of passion and purpose.

the world can understand. Mother Teresa has fed millions, both physically and spiritually.

If Colin Powell succeeds in his mission to recruit lean-and-mean companies to spare money, time, and people to attack social problems during the workday, we'll have even greater opportunities to put passion back into the workplace. But whether his volunteerism crusade lasts or wanes, women as individuals can incorporate meaning into their lives and rejuvenate their own spirit by their own impetus.

Fame or no fame, reward or no reward, women have opportunity to invest in the future by making a spiritual connection with others for purposes outside themselves. For Debbie Henderson, it's her involvement as a Girl Scout leader to build girls' character and faith. For Barbara Durand, it's events and career counseling to job seekers. For Sue Morris, it's sitting on the advisory board of a foundation that helps abused children. To Linda Bates Parker, it means spearheading the career and placement efforts at the University of Cincinnati, and community initiatives for young African-American males and leadership training for African-American executives. For Kathy Anfuso, daughter of Bill Shay, for whom Shay Stadium was named, it's hospitality to those in need.

We all do "nice things" for people from time to time. The point is, we don't do them often enough. Having a formal commitment helps. If you know you have someone, or a group of someones, waiting for you, that can often be the catalyst you need when the time commitment really becomes a sacrifice.

There was a time about five or six years ago that my speaking schedule required that I be out of town many weekends. So it became harder and harder to be a part of an organized effort to "give back" to the community and the church. It was about that same time that I began to feel "weighted down" with the routine of my job and uncertain that my work really mattered. That's when I made a conscious effort to practice this principle again in my life — to commit to a project that really mattered for the long haul.

My husband and I took some of our communication principles that we teach for corporate clients and repackaged them into a seminar for married couples. After we finished the "creation" process, we had a 26-week course for couples beginning second marriages and blended families — everything from listening skills to conflict resolution to romance to communication with ex-spouses and ex-in-laws over discipline issues.

We started by inviting newlywed or newly engaged couples to our home on Saturday evenings once a month for a seminar session and dessert. Later we incorporated the series into our church's educational program. Sure, it can be tough week in and week out to meet a schedule for preparation and delivery, but the rewards of "up-ing" the success rate of second marriages has re-created the passion for the communication skills that had become "routine" for corporate audiences.

*Smart women
...replenish their
spirit by investing
emotional energy
and time in a cause
that serves a
larger purpose.*

In short, the work rejuvenates my spirit. It makes a difference, a difference that I can see in couples' lives week to week.

Smart women have learned the value of personal involvement. They replenish their spirit by investing emotional energy and time in a cause that serves a larger purpose. They have become contributors, not spectators. As a result, they have gained a deep sense of fulfillment. One by one, we all make a difference for two or three.

Recognize God's Presence When You See It

Some women push for proof. They look to studies and research published in reputable scientific and medical journals, like the article recently published in *Journal of Obstetric, Gynecologic and Neonatal Nursing.* The article reports that a woman's spirituality can contribute to positive health behaviors and help her cope with health complications. The study defines spirituality as belief in something greater than self and a faith that positively affirms life.

Research can't fully explain the mind-body connection, but surveys indicate that spirituality and faith play an important part in how a woman experiences health and sickness — her own or that of others she loves. Researchers suggest several explanations: her faith leads her to more healthful lifestyle choices, such as avoiding smoking or drugs. Prayer helps her manage stress and anxiety. Faith boosts her emotional energy to cope with life's challenges. Those feelings of faith often increase self-esteem, release creative energy, and empower her to act. Her faith cultivates inner calm.

Without a doubt, that faith has been my own source of strength and direction through the years. At age 27, with two small children, I began to understand that my husband's future was highly unstable. The probability that I would be supporting us loomed large. I had accepted a teaching job, but felt restless and bored after the first year. I had published one article for a small magazine, and the editor asked if I'd take on a short series of assignments. The payment was a pittance, but more importantly, it was encouragement that someone saw an inkling of talent in my writing. For weeks I vacillated between the "security" of a teacher's paycheck and my passion for writing.

My husband had just come home from his first hospitalization, and fear of what the future held for us financially haunted me. For three nights I lay awake staring at the ceiling. What to do? Resign my teaching job to take the writing assignment or hold on to the steady check? Weary from lack of sleep and worry over the way the medication was affecting my husband, I got out of bed at three in the morning, padded into the family room, opened my Bible, and thought, "God, I've got to have an answer. I'll take either a yes or a no. But I've gotta have an answer. I'm desperate. I need to sleep."

Write. A peace came over me as strongly as if someone had draped a blanket around my shoulders. I closed my Bible, got up and padded back into the bedroom, and promptly fell sound asleep. The next morning I walked into my principal's office and resigned my job.

"Well," he said, "I hate to hear that. But your timing couldn't be better; there's a school board meeting tonight. So

Those feelings of faith often increase self-esteem, release creative energy, and empower her to act.

if you'll write out your resignation, I'll go ahead and present it to the board so they can act on it right away. That way, you can make it effective at midterm." Relieved that the decision was over and the deed done, I scurried off for the day.

The next morning as I drove to school, I flipped on the car radio to hear the local news in our small town. Then this announcement riveted my attention: "The school board met last night in its monthly meeting, and in rather unusual action, they voted *not* to accept Spanish teacher Dianna Booher's resignation." What? What? But I thought.... All the serenity of the previous day slipped out of my body.

When I pulled into the school parking lot, I headed straight for the principal's office. "What's going on? I've never heard of a school board refusing to let someone out of their contract?"

"Neither have I," the principal acknowledged. "The problem is, they don't have anybody else qualified to teach Spanish. Not a single applicant. And Pampa's such a small town. What are the chances they can get someone in here by midterm?" It wasn't really a question, but a statement. He continued, "So I'm sorry. It looks like you'll have to finish out the year with us."

Confusion. What now? Why the feeling that my purpose was to write, and then suddenly this change of events? Another few sleepless nights.

Four days later, I got a note from the principal to stop by his office before I left for the day. When I walked in, he wore a broad smile. "We just got a call from a woman planning to move back here to take care of her elderly mother who's sick. She wants a teaching job. Spanish."

And that was that. The end of teaching school. The beginning of a writing career.

Through the years as a writer and small business owner, that situation has repeated itself in a thousand ways. My faith has given me direction, comfort, and serenity. It is my grounding when all the world around me sways.

Though they may not be able to explain fully the hows and whys, smart women recognize evidence of God's presence when they see it and feel it. Like Brother Roger of Taize has observed: "It is never our faith that creates God, nor is it our doubts that put an end to God's existence."

Smart women come to recognize God's presence in the world in different ways.

One wife says it was trouble in her marriage and a brief separation from her husband that focused her on the spiritual vacuum in her life: "When he moved out for a period of time, I felt like the foundation had been knocked out from underneath me. I was adrift. That's when I really became a believer. And I think God allowed that so I would shift my foundation, so to speak, from Doug to Him.

"I had tried spending time with friends, and I tried talking it through with people. I tried talking it through with a shrink. Spiritually speaking, I tried the world. But there was no depth. There were no deep answers; it was all superficial. When I turned to the Bible, I just looked up all the scriptures on love and all the scriptures on how to be a wife, and on and on. I spent hours praying. God shifted my attention to the fact that I needed to change myself. God would take care of Doug; my project was me."

Smart women come to recognize God's presence in the world in different ways.

On the other hand, some women recognize God's presence through a satisfying marriage: "I've been very grateful because it [marriage] is very enriching. I am fortunate enough to share my beliefs with my husband, and that's a priceless thing — to be in a marriage where you have a similar spiritual bond and walk together."

Some women recognize God's presence only when their children's lives are affected. Very confident, capable women can be brought to their knees when they have a wayward child and become fearful for that child's safety or future. What we endure for ourselves, we cannot endure for our children.

Barbara Durand sensed that helplessness during her son's spine surgery for scoliosis: "As a Christian mom, I thought I had surrendered my children to the Lord and trusted Him to meet their needs, but there was an incredible sense of helplessness for a while, grappling with that, recognizing the pain that this child was going to go through in surgery — and the potential risk. I felt totally powerless to do anything about it. So in those significant times in my life I've just been reminded that I am not in control. And I am content with that."

For some women, it's the process of building relationships that leads them to recognize God's presence.

Relationships are a lot like ravioli. Can you visualize a big plate of ravioli just now? Those lumps of pasta wrapped around those delicious centers of soft cheese. And they're all floating in that thick, well-seasoned tomato sauce. Relationships in our life resemble those bites of pasta. They're the main event. We fork into them with gusto because they fill our time and our appetites. Incorporated into our life, they make us feel full and satisfied. But where would those lumps of pasta be without the sauce they're floating in? Stranded on the plate, dry, tasteless.

The sauce that flavors all relationships is our sense of spiritual connection — common values and beliefs that hold our lives together in one harmonious dish. When we don't have that connection, we find relationships with certain people dry and difficult.

Katy Crane says, "I think the whole goal in life — one of those great truths — is to be intimate with people. There's a deep yearning for that. Of course, the real true yearning is to be intimate with God, but sometimes that starts with people. And you can't get to intimacy without going through honesty and transparency. One of the biggest revelations to me is that everybody's the same! It really doesn't matter whether you're a bum on Bernside or the Queen of England, we are all the same. It has given me more confidence in relationships because I now know that. Regardless of whatever front people put on, they have the same deep needs that I have."

For some women, recognizing God's presence is just a growing awareness, brought on by nothing in particular. One woman given to philosophy expresses it this way: "What I have found out in my first half a century is that for me, God is law. It's very, very clear, an easy way for me to understand cause and effect. There is law and order in this universe. There is cause and effect. There is divine order. There is right action.

And when you stay within the confines of what that law is, life works. Once I figured that out, then I found love, peace, joy, and prosperity."

And there are seekers — those still looking for evidence of God's presence in the world and in their personal lives.

One interviewee explains her spiritual journey this way: "I haven't really decided what spirituality is for me. I'm still grappling with that. But I'm very philosophical. I think about these things a lot, but less in a traditional sense than other people probably. Actually, I would like to have more of a sense of that side of my life. It would be easier for me to just go someplace and gain some comfort from either a sermon or a priest. Mine [nature] is more to challenge that, to want to discuss it, so I have a lot of philosophical discussions."

One other admitted seeker summed up: "I no longer practice any religion, but I consider myself spiritual. I guess the overall understanding is that I'm a human being, a member of the human race, and there's a humility about me. I know there's something greater than that. I don't know what it is. I see my life as a gift that I'm using. I don't really understand it. It's a mystery. But I just know that there's something beyond what I can see and what I can feel and what I can touch. There's another dimension — there's just too much stuff out there that you cannot explain except for the feeling that it's the spiritual. Whatever it is, life isn't just us."

The majority of smart women are seeking the deeper dimension in life.

The majority of smart women are seeking the deeper dimension in life.

Know When to Let Go

Smart, successful women master their moods. They have a sense of self-worth. They set sail on their own seas, driven by their own goals. They take risks. They make difficult decisions. They put up or shut up. They ask for feedback and do course corrections. They build strong relationships. They make deliberate, ethical choices.

That's why the spiritual realm sometimes perplexes them. Part of spiritual awareness involves acknowledging our *lack* of ultimate control in life and acknowledging God's presence in the universe and in our lives.

A friend once passed on this insight she'd heard from someone: God doesn't come to take sides, but to take control. Often in relationships that are breaking our hearts, we plead for God to fix things. We want a husband stopped, a child calmed, an in-law reprimanded, or a coworker zapped into shape.

But when God acts or intervenes in our life, He doesn't just take on our role of nagger, nurturer, or neighbor. He sees the entire situation and takes control for the good of us all. Those who welcome Him into their lives welcome His control and trust His goodness. Those who shut Him out mentally and emotionally continue to try to keep their ship afloat and then complain that He didn't intervene when they were about to drown.

One interviewee tells about her agonizing conflict with the judicial system until she emotionally and willfully relinquished the control she never really had over the situation. With a small daughter in tow, Elaine left a physically abusive husband. But that was before she realized the power of a crooked judge in a small town. Her angry ex-husband fought to regain custody of their daughter, a pawn in the battle with his wife. Although Elaine soon met and married a wonderful Christian man who wanted to adopt her young daughter, the angry biological father fought to have the custody decision reversed and reclaim his "possession."

Later, the truth came out. This particular judge *always* ruled in favor of fathers in his courtroom, and a particular lawyer *always* represented these fathers. The racket that soon unfolded under investigation was kickbacks to the judge and referrals to the lawyer from a nearby corporation to its employees needing legal assistance.

In the midst of this agonizing battle for her daughter, Elaine came to recognize God's presence and control only when she relinquished hers. Up to that point, she and her new husband had been fighting in court for the daughter's future.

She says, "We had a struggle between the biological father and mother. I was saying, 'I know what is best for my

Part of spiritual awareness involves acknowledging our lack of ultimate control in life and acknowledging God's presence in the universe and in our lives.

child — I want her with me.' On the other side, he was saying, 'I am stealing my daughter from you.' Finally, I came to the point of saying, 'You know, God, if You think she's going to do best with him, that's Your decision. I cannot determine what a judge will do. You, God, do know. And if You say she will be best with her father, even though I would just die, You take her and You give her to him.' When I finally, earnestly, prayed that prayer, her biological father said to the judge, 'I don't ever want to see her [the child] again.' "

For some people, "control" in anybody else's hands becomes frightening. In their experience, control has been a measure of personal and career success, so they resist having to give it up — even to a Higher Power. They have a sense of themselves as successful people with important careers and positions. Control drives their thought process. They control their life as they control their calendar. They base their self-image on the picture of themselves they see scattered across their desk. Common thinking goes something like this: I have a to-do list that's full. I have a calendar that's full. I have many e-mails waiting. I have people and projects waiting for my approval. Therefore, I am in control."

Recognizing God's ultimate control means surrendering our own control. That sense of fear or calm at acknowledging God's control depends on our understanding of God's nature: Do we see God as an angry, capricious God or a loving, concerned God? The large majority of smart women interviewed have staked their lives on a concerned, personal God.

The large majority of smart women interviewed have staked their lives on a concerned, personal God.

Centering Yourself With Spiritual Certainties

Anyone alive in our century has come to realize the vastness of our universe and how much there is to know about it. Any thinking human being understands that what we know about our brain, our body, and our spirit is still in its infancy.

But that overwhelming thought is much like the technology of the Internet. The fundamental nature of how our words travel over cable to the other side of the world is almost beyond comprehension. Yet we know that it happens.

Most thinking people are beginning to discover that although they may not grasp the full concept of our spiritual universe, they know it exists. They see lives and situations change because of God's work in the world.

Seventy-three percent of the women interviewed called themselves believers and referred to a personal relationship with God. An additional 16 percent said they believed in a Higher Power and described themselves as seeking to know more and experience more of the spiritual realm in life. Only 11 percent of those interviewed did not believe in a Higher Power. And the higher the education, the more likely they were to categorize themselves as believers. Here are the spiritual certainties claimed by these smart women:

God Loves Me: From an organizational-development consultant: "Finally, I did some reading and talking with other people, and then just sat down with myself and said, 'If God is Who God is supposed to be, there has to be more to this than these black-and-white rules. I don't know what it is or what's out there, but I'm just going to take this leap of faith here and move forward.' I think that at that point I dropped out of *religion* and found *spirituality*. My prayer life took a whole different turn at that point. It's a very freeing thing to know there is Someone Who cares for me."

And the higher the education, the more likely they were to categorize themselves as believers.

From a senior executive: "When I make myself more available to God and don't overplan my life, then I see more truth than when I chart it very carefully. This for me has been a maturing thing — to have enough confidence to do that. To be comfortable with who I am. I do have confidence because I know that God loves me. I know that. So I don't have a big need to keep proving myself."

God Has a Plan for My Life: From a Ph.D. director of nursing: "I think it's a relationship with God, not a religion. I think it's important to take time away and think, 'What is your purpose here? Why were you created? What is the great, grand design of your life?' To me, to think that career is that grand design is just too limiting. We have so much potential in so many areas; career is just one facet of that. I love to read the Bible, particularly the New Testament. And I like to read about giants in Christian literature that really effected a change in countries or in their area of the world through what they did in ministry."

God Gives Me Wisdom: From an entrepreneur: "My faith is so real to me. When I lost my earthly father, I became very close to my Heavenly Father. I can deal with day-to-day business when I have my Father. I do not leave my house in the morning without saying a prayer, 'God, get me through this day. Give me discernment, wisdom. This company is Yours. Help me run it as You would have me run it.' I couldn't have said this three years ago, but I was in a comfy situation then. Now I am stronger."

From a former lawyer and nurse and now stay-at-home mom: "Through prayer and faith, I have been guided. If I didn't have that faith, who would be guiding me? Being fiercely independent and having a sense of adventure in my earlier career and while I was single, I still had God to lean on and His Word to refer to. I find that being in fellowship with other Christians gives me constant role models if I ever am weak or lose focus."

God Gives Me Companionship: From a senior manager: "No one's ever going to shake my beliefs from me — once I finally figured out what they are. The temptation is just not to nurture that relationship with God — it can't just go on automatic pilot. To me, my faith is knowing that God is always there and there's no circumstance I can't get through. There's companionship there, there's camaraderie, even in the darkest moments. It's that faith that you're not by yourself in this life, that you're not facing this alone. It is the sense of knowing you are safe."

God Controls My Future: A middle manager says: "My certainty is knowing that my personal Lord and Savior will never leave or forsake me. It is knowing that life simply isn't about me, my husband, and my family. We are all components of life, but there is a great governing power that holds it all together. With faith in Him, there is eternal salvation. We will live forever eternally."

God Gives Me Peace: From a Ph.D. author: "My faith is

the absolute rock. It's my foundation. My time-saver. My energy builder. What I turn to when other things don't work. It's my default, my center."

A middle manager: "My faith is the foundation for my life. It gives all of life meaning. It gives you more happiness, more understanding. When we got married the preacher said, 'Your joy will be doubled and your pain halved.' That's the same with faith in God."

From another entrepreneur: "I work like a Trojan during the day, but when it comes time for me to go to sleep, I never have any problems sleeping. I sleep so soundly. I think that's because I have inner peace."

From a middle manager: "I went to church when I was small, but when my mother stopped going, I stopped. When I came to this job, the man who hired me got me going to his church. That's when I became a Christian. I'm trying to teach my kids that it's such a peaceful place to be. It's like an anchor that can help you find your place, no matter what else is going on around you. I can turn 360 degrees and go any direction, but I am anchored there. I feel good about that. It gives me a rock in my life that's not turning over or moving."

And finally, here is the certainty for one seventy-six-year-old Ph.D.: "In 1951 — I was thirty — I started daily quiet time with God. My life is in two parts — before and after that time. It's still a part of my life. That determined daily quiet time with God has made all the difference."

God Uses Me to Influence Others: From an attorney: "The other part is sharing my spiritual journey with other co-soul-journers. I get a special pleasure from talking with people who are curious, but are also understandably threatened by investigating spirituality because they've been so wounded trying to explore things before. I like building enough trust so we can begin to talk about it."

From a Ph.D. and nurse: "I'm a born-again Christian. As a result of that, I am here and alive for a purpose. Part of that purpose is to lead my children, my friends, and my associates to further their own spirituality and their maturity. I want to be an example of how to treat other people with compassion."

An insurance executive: "I was the number one person hired to build this business. I am the leader and mentor to these people here. It's really important to me that they are able to see something different about me. Different in the way I respond. Different in the way I handle situations. It's not always easy, in corporate situations, but sometimes you can lead by example, by the way you conduct your life."

Smart women have built their lives on these spiritual certainties. They feel centered, serene, and content to let God have control in their lives.

Live Today Without Losing Sight of Tomorrow

Peter Drucker, still the most acclaimed management and business philosopher of our time, recalls the influence a conversation with famous economist Joseph Schumpeter had on his life back in 1949. Drucker says he learned from it three things: First, one has to ask one's self what he or she wants to be remembered for. Second, that idea should change. And third, one thing worth being remembered for is the difference one makes in the lives of other people." (Adapted from *Drucker on Asia: The Drucker-Nakauchi Dialogue, 1996)*

Susan, mother of two young teens, understood that. Although I have never met Susan myself, her friend Debbie Shaw Hertzog wrote this letter to her shortly before her death. Her family asked that it be part of her eulogy.

Smart women have built their lives on these spiritual certainties. They feel centered, serene, and content to let God have control in their lives.

January 25, 1997
Dear Susan,

You have been in the prayers of so many during your courageous battle. Your strong spirit touched me from the first time I met you at Living Word [church]. I was certain I had met a kindred spirit. We had so much in common, and how I hoped for the opportunity to be friends. I am so grateful for the times we did have to visit and share.

Most of all, our recent conversation after Christmas about the importance of being centered. I thought, this incredible woman is advising me on the importance of staying centered and focused, regardless of the adversities that come into our life. There I was dealing only with the hassles of the holidays, too much PTA work, the frustrations of home and family and being pulled in a thousand different directions. And you, Susan, challenged with sickness, yet tough and strong, and able still to rise above it and be the one in control. Thank you for your insight and wisdom. I took it to heart and have shared it with others.

...As Christians, we can take comfort in knowing that our soul remains unharmed and in God's hands. We can find peace knowing that He has a plan for our life and.... We are...to trust.

Many years ago when I was in the play, "The Shadow Box," inspired by the book, **Death, the Final Stage of Growth**, by Dr. Elizabeth Kubler-Ross, I learned many powerful things. I played the part of Maggie, whose husband was in a hospice. The author shared this: "What is important is to realize that whether we understand fully why we are here or what will happen when we die, it is our purpose as human beings to continue to grow, to look within ourselves, to find and to build upon that source of peace and understanding and strength which is our inner selves. Then to reach out one to another in love, acceptance, in patient guidance, and hope for what we may all become together."

I admire you for having been able to do just this. I am sure you have inspired many people other than me with your strength and determination. Please know how thankful I am that our paths crossed that morning at church. I look forward to getting to know your children better, and Scott as well. The Living Word family is there for them. Susan, God is with you and you are in the hearts and minds of the many who love you.

Your friend,
Debbie

Susan left an imprint on her friend's heart. Smart women want to have an impact on their friends and family in memorable ways. Life for them is about spiritual connections deeper than earthly bonds.

To do that, we have to recognize that today's minutes count. At one period of my life, I seemed to be frantically rushing from one activity to the next. A friend asked, "Why are you rushing through life? Are you in a hurry to get to the end?" It was quite a sobering question to me.

Life happens on the way to the future. Similar to calendars, smart women see their lives from two perspectives: "a day at a glance" and "a lifetime at a glance." If we keep our calendars open only to the "lifetime at a glance" view, we forget to live each day to its fullest. We skip meaningful moments because we seem to be hurrying to turn the page.

On the other hand, if we leave our calendars open only to "day at a glance," we may miss reminders that the sum of our life is our days end to end. Both calendar views give us the complete perspective. Our total impact on family, friends, and associates will amount to our impact one day at a time.

Living life to the fullest now doesn't mean that we do not plan for the future. On the contrary, we invest ourselves in things and people that have a life beyond ours. But living today means we can live with the confidence that actions today affect the quality and peace in our lives for years to come, though probably not so dramatically foreshadowed as to one interviewee:

Smart women want to have an impact on their friends and family in memorable ways. Life for them is about spiritual connections deeper than earthly bonds.

In chapter 8, interviewee Tricia recalled the ongoing difficulty with her adopted teenage son. Ten years before he returned to her home a last time, in the midst of their struggle, she had what she calls a "waking dream." Driving along in the car, she saw the inside of a church — one unfamiliar to her — and her teenage son standing before the church, giving his testimony and renewing his commitment to God. She spoke aloud during that waking dream to her husband, "I wonder what he will say about me?"

Despite her anxiety about her son's answer to that question during their troubled relationship, that was God's reassurance, she insists, that things would eventually work out with her son. Ten years later, when she saw her son standing in front of her literal church, telling about the change God had made in his life, she recalled the waking dream ten years earlier. "It was just so amazing — to think there is this common thread. That's faith, the spiritual realm. You may not see it, but it's there. I am not alone."

Generally speaking, we feel separated from God in two situations: when we have plenty and when we have little. When we have plenty — money, job, friends, good times — we somehow think they have all come about by our own efforts and wisdom. When we have little — no money, no job, no friends, tragedy, and disappointment — we feel that God has pulled away from us and no longer cares. But smart women think differently.

Smart women have given a great deal of thought to their spiritual nature.

Smart women have a personal relationship with God that gives them a heart of gratitude in "feast" and a steadfast peace and hope during "famine."

Smart women have given a great deal of thought to their spiritual nature. That thought creates their calm center and motivates their outward action, producing high impact in the lives of others. They have anchored themselves on spiritual certainties in life. They have found answers, purpose, and meaning for their lives in their faith.

10
Swim in the Seasons of Life

S ome of us have been swimming upstream in the frigid water of winter all our lives. In youth, we want to be grown up, married, and dancing in Carnegie Hall for millions before we learn to balance ourselves on one toe. In young adulthood, we want to earn millions and live in a mansion before we learn to balance our bank account against booties and braces. In middle age, we experience a crisis of commitment that leads us to end our marriages before we examine our own goals and character. Then in maturity, we long for the energy and health of youth and a fresh start on decisions more properly made earlier in life.

Decisions, duties, and devotions are a lot like bananas, strawberries, and avocados — a lot more expensive out of season. At best, they cost more money, time, and trouble than they should. At worst, they are beyond our reach.

There is a time

for everything...

According to the writer of Ecclesiastes in the Bible:

There is a time for everything,
And a season for every activity under heaven:
A time to be born, and a time to die,
A time to plant, and a time to uproot,
A time to kill, and a time to heal;
A time to break down, and a time to build up;
A time to weep, and a time to laugh;
A time to mourn, and a time to dance;

A time to scatter stones, and a time to gather them,

A time to embrace, and a time to refrain,

A time to search, and a time to give up,

A time to keep, and a time to throw away;

A time to tear, and time to mend,

A time to keep silent, and a time to speak,

A time to love, and a time to hate;

A time of war, and a time of peace.

Ecclesiastes 3:1-8 (New International Version)

Smart women learn to swim with the seasons of life. They understand that each season of life has its own commitments and joys. They swim with the current in warm weather and enjoy the experience.

Out-of-Season Thinking in Youth

Smart women learn to swim with the seasons of life.

As teenagers, we are often pushed out of our innocence. Parents may intentionally or unintentionally rip childhood from us, forcing us to fend for ourselves with neither physical nor emotional support. On the other hand, nurturing parents may have provided advantages, comforts, and stability, but for some reason, we ourselves may have felt the need to get on with our lives — away from their guidance and control. We may feel the pull of the exciting unknown in a culture that permits youthful experimentation about choices that might be better made in later years under different circumstances.

Whichever the case, swimming out of season as teens leads us to shun an education, marry too early, or choose a job that puts food on our tables but does not feed our souls.

For any number of reasons, some teens thrash around in the cool spring temperatures against the current. They arrive at adulthood feeling uncomfortable, unprepared, and unaccepted.

In-Season Thinking As a Youth

Some teenagers swim with the current in the spring time. The cool water provides just enough exhilaration so that they enjoy a close relationship with loving parents who offer acceptance, guidance, and encouragement. They have enough money to meet their physical needs. They learn to value education. They have opportunities to participate in many activities that expand their interests. They learn from friends how to get along with other people.

They feel loved by their families, important in the world, and excited about assuming their later role as wives, mothers, daughters, friends, partners, employees, or employers.

These teens splash around in the springtime, loving every minute of sunshine.

Out-of-Season Thinking as a Young Adult

Young adults swimming out of season begin to think they are not moving along fast enough. They feel weighted down by the responsibilities of young children and the dictates of bad bosses. They grow weary of midnight earaches, soccer practice on Saturdays, and affordable vacations to Grandma's. They feel resentment that their spouse is pouring little effort into the relationship and financial foundation. They feel jealous that their parents or friends have bigger houses, longer vacations, higher promotions, and more toys.

They begin to push, pull, then shove and yank on themselves or their spouse for not swimming faster into their future and fortune.

These teens splash around in the spring time, loving every minute of sunshine.

In-Season Thinking as a Young Adult

Young adults swimming in the summertime understand that sacrifice and hard work build character. They make room for children in their lives. They enjoy hearing their laughter and healing their lumps and bumps. They start planting seeds of friendship that will bear fruit immediately and again later. They gather on-the-job experiences as "tools" for their self-development kits, knowing that any specific job may come or go.

They watch their parents' generation to learn from their mistakes and failures with careers, families, and lifestyles. They forgive themselves for adolescent mistakes, overlook parents for their shortcomings, and permit their kids to be kids. They adapt. They get out of the stream occasionally to look around. Sometimes they change directions and head for another bank that looks more rewarding.

The sunshine, the freedom, the exhilaration of the swim — that's what this season of life is all about.

Out-of-Season Thinking in Middle Age

Women in their forties, fifties, and sixties may still be swimming out of season, against the current. They blame elderly parents, vindictive bosses, or wayward children for restricting their lives and limiting their choices. They have parents who demand attention when they didn't give it earlier in life. They have children who demand more and more and threaten to withdraw the relationship or grandchildren if their wishes aren't met. They have bosses who say, shape up or start over at the bottom of the heap.

The sunshine, the freedom, the exhilaration of the swim — that's what this season of life is all about.

They fear this might be their last fling before winter sets in. In the fall of life, these women conclude that it's too early for the leaves to fall. Instead of marveling at the rich colors of so many choices, they are angry about the crop they are harvesting. Or, they are frustrated about the limitations they face in replanting out of season. The rain is too heavy and too frequent. The soil seems used up and hard. The first freeze brings fear.

They feel caught in a current that is sweeping them downstream faster and faster without letting them lift their head out of the water long enough to enjoy the view. They are tired, disappointed, and distressed that they are caught in a performance trap and drowning in family and financial obligations.

In-Season Thinking in Middle Age

These midlifers are swimming along with the current in the fall of life with great confidence. They are not in such a big hurry to move downstream as they are wanting to make sure they enjoy each babbling brook and shady picnic cove along the way. They no longer feel the frantic scare as they drop over a new waterfall along the way. They no longer feel weighed down by spouses and children. Instead, they find those spouses and children make the trip more enjoyable. These women often invite their family to swim alongside of them just for the conversation.

They plan to savor the last few years with their elderly parents, to heal old wounds, to build new bridges, to learn from their insights.

They feel security in their careers, if not in their current jobs, then in their ability to learn and earn for a lifetime.

As for the pocketbooks, they want enough — not too much that would handcuff them to a lifetime of work — not too little that would make them dependent on others. They have found deeper waters and stronger anchors in life than a paycheck, an industry plaque, or a home in the suburbs.

They enjoy climbing up on the bank from time to time to help someone else find direction in life. The sunshine no longer beats down on them. They welcome shade trees of protection, shorter days of work, piling leaves of interests, and the rich color of relationships with family and friends.

They enjoy climbing up on the bank from time to time to help someone else find direction in life.

Out-of-Season Thinking at Maturity

Out-of-season swimmers in the dead of winter fear for their lives. They feel cold, dehydrated, and mistreated. They fear that their values and relationships will not be able to sustain them until the end comes. They feel unsure of friendships, wondering if they will last when hard times come. They despise what age has done to their energy and outlook. They have stopped swimming too soon and feel helpless to tread water.

They watch laughing young people spill over the waterfalls and long to run free with them once again. Their eyes fill with regret about the friendships they didn't make and the family they didn't have time for. They feel bitter that their jobs didn't provide a better living, that their missions didn't provide a sense of accomplishment, and that their goals didn't lead to a different destination.

In-Season Thinking at Maturity

Those who have reached the beautiful beach have dried themselves off after leaving the water. They feel invigorated by the swim, cozy by the fire, nourished by the hot chocolate, proud of the accomplishments, and needed by those who are still asking for direction along the route.

Who wants to swim in cold water in the dead of winter? Not these swimmers. They enjoyed the thrashing around of their youth, the thrill of the rapids in young adulthood, and the sunshine and shade of middle-age. But now they are content to reap the rewards of wisdom in maturity from a life well lived, surrounded by people well loved.

Reflections on the Seasons of Life

One woman remembers the pressure she felt as a teen in trying to swim upstream and excel beyond her years and capabilities: "I am an only child, and I sensed that my parents were living out their lives vicariously through me, looking to me to achieve many of the things they did not have an opportunity to do. As I child, I felt they had expectations that I would excel in a lot of areas and make them proud and make them feel that they had succeeded as parents. That was a big order for me to fill. I felt that no matter what I did, I would let them down in some area. As I matured, I realized that a lot of that [pressure] was just really my perception. My parents loved me very much and were probably very accepting of who I was, but I got into a performance trap. So without ever acting it out, I went through a quiet rebellion against what I thought were their expectations."

Another successful woman tells about derailing her life because of a pregnancy in the wrong season of life: "I've had a couple of major detours in my life, one was when I was 17. I became pregnant. I had this golden high school career going. I was headed off to England to study, but I was kicked out of the National Honor Society. Then they wouldn't let me be in the school play. That was a major derailment. It was a real attack on my self-esteem. It made me less sure of myself for a long time."

...they are content to reap the rewards of wisdom in maturity from a life well lived, surrounded by people well loved.

Another executive tells about teaching her college-age sons about the seasons of life: "Sometimes when children are in school, they get really frustrated. They can't see beyond school and they're sick of it. But I try to say to them, 'This is your job now. This is what you're to do now. The other will follow.' This has been a maturing thing for me — I haven't always thought this way. I recognize there are seasons, and the Lord willing, I will have opportunity for things that I dream about later. It's just not the right time now. So I just say, 'Okay, I'm so thankful that I'm able to do what I do now, and I'll be able to do that eventually."

Another interviewee talks about growing to be comfortable in a new season of life: "I have gotten more comfortable with being by myself as I've gotten older. I used to be unable to be alone. I hated it. But that was in those days when I was looking for someone else to define me. Now, I'm much more comfortable with solitude. I know myself a little better."

Another woman talks about her season as the supportive wife through her husband's career change: "I held the top sales position in order of volume, but when Ed began to do some consulting work, I began to take a less active role. I knew in my heart of hearts that we were probably going to be making a move. My first obligation and duty was to be his wife, and so I said, 'Right now, I think you need me more than I need to be performing for myself.' So I supported him in some of his efforts. I slowed down tremendously in prospecting, which is the root of my business, as well as referrals, so I could be available to help him."

A middle manager talks about adapting dreams to significant others in her life: "I put aside some of my career goals when my family came along. I was not willing to do the travel, or go take a one-year assignment, or move to another city. So I put my career on a sidetrack. It's still really important to me, but my family comes first."

From talking with these and other women and from my own experience, I sense that the two seasons of life that produce the most restlessness and fear are those involving parenting small children and growing older.

I remember the boredom of having to stay in bed for five months during my second pregnancy. Later, during one particular stretch of childhood illnesses when both children had the measles, then colds, and then ear infections, I stayed indoors for a full six weeks before they were well enough to go places again. I remember the fear with which I walked back into the classroom to teach Spanish for my first year as a teacher, having been out of college for six years without so much as looking at a lesson plan. Had my brain atrophied? Would I remember the vocabulary at all? Was my teaching certificate even valid anymore?

And now I'm into a new season of life: My daughter had my first grandchild, Mason, five months ago. As I write this book now in my hotel room in Washington, D.C., holed up between speaking engagements, Room Service just knocked on my door with dessert. When I told the waiter he had the wrong room, he said, "No, your daughter just called to ask us to deliver it quickly before you went to bed. He handed me a card off the tray. It said, "Don't work too hard. I miss you. Love, Mason."

the two seasons of life that produce the most restlessness and fear are those involving parenting small children and growing older.

Enjoying my strawberries and blackberries swimming in caramel sauce, scenes of the last five months flashed before my eyes: First, the day Lisa checked into the hospital. She had an unexpected difficulty that first hour of labor during which a team of blue coats swarmed around her bed. Although I sat with her and my son-in-law in the delivery room for the rest of the morning, nothing could prepare me for the final hour of agony I spent outside her door, waiting in the last few moments before I heard Mason's first cry.

Then there was the night I started to pack my clothes to go home after spending that first week with them to help with the new baby. She'd gone through the usual post-partem depression silently, but that night she tiptoed into the bedroom, tears streaming down her face. "Please, Mother, can you stay another day or two? I'm just not ready. What if I can't take care of him? What if something happens to him and I don't know what to do?"

How well I understood the overwhelming fear of feeling totally responsible for a helpless baby. I took her in my arms and tried to reassure her that this feeling, too, would pass.

Although I didn't have the heart to tell her then, I knew that her years of fear and exhaustion were just beginning. That night as I rocked Mason between midnight and morning, the various scenes of his mother's own childhood and that of her older brother, Jeff, drifted through my mind.

There was the time Lisa, at age three, had crawled up on a breakfast stool at the bar and bumped my arm just as I was transferring a pot of boiling beans from the cooking range to the table. The hot juice splashed on her cheek and produced a big blister before we could get her to the emergency room.

Then there was the time when, as a toddler, she found the empty ammonia bottle in the trash bag, sitting beside the back door to be taken outside. She'd taken a whiff from the remaining fumes, couldn't get her breath, turned blue, and passed out.

There was the day both Jeff and Lisa were "helping" me clean upstairs and downstairs closets. Jeff, at four, had taken an electric hot-plate from the upstairs to the downstairs closet for me — except he took things one step further and plugged the hot-plate into a wall socket. Toddler Lisa placed her plastic tea set on it, and when the plate got hot, it burst into flames. Two minutes later, when I walked into the bedroom with my armload of toys from the upstairs closet, there was a three-foot fire in the center of the room. Both kids, with sooty faces, stood in wide-eyed amazement at what they had accomplished in two minutes.

There was the night I came home from a parent-teacher conference that first year of teaching and found Jeff and his dad on the way to the hospital. Jeff had fallen and cracked open his head on the corner of the bed while playing cowboys and needed stitches.

There was the day Jeff ran in from the playground with a trail of kids following him and yelling, "Jeff got a stick in his eye! Jeff got a stick in his eyes! He's bleeding bad. He's bleeding bad!" Sure enough, he'd run into a tree limb that missed his eyeball about one-eighth of an inch. Off we went to the hospital and the plastic surgeon for a miraculous repair job that left no scar.

Then there was the day Lisa broke her foot jumping on the trampoline, and the day Jeff twisted his knee so severely during a seventh-grade football game that he had to have surgery.

But the worst nightmare of all was the summer day I had dashed into a department store, leaving both kids in the car. Lisa, at about six months, was sound asleep in her car seat, the old kind from which you had to wake them from a good sleep to remove them. Jeff, at two-and-half, was quietly playing in the back seat. I don't remember the purpose of my errand that day, but so as not to disturb them, I locked them safely inside the car and dashed into the store, from where I could keep my eye on them at all times. What I didn't realize was how hot the Texas sun could make the car in a matter of minutes.

When I returned to the car, I'll never forget the scene. It is imprinted on my mind forever. Both kids looked up at me, limp and lifeless, sweat dripping from their faces and hair. As soon as I unlocked the door and let in the air, they perked up. I never realized the true danger until years later when I saw a television news report of a child who'd died in similar conditions. My tears well up and I get a knot in my stomach every time I think of my ignorance as a twenty-four-year-old mother.

Yes, the seasons change. As I sit here enjoying my dessert that "five-month-old grandson Mason" ordered for me, I'm so grateful for two things: the opportunity and miracle I had to enjoy my children grow up, and the opportunity I have to hug and hold my grandson.

In this newest season of life, I can let my daughter deal with all the fears that come from mothering normally active children for the next eighteen years. As for me, I can hug my grandson, play with him, buy him presents, and then leave to go shopping without a stroller or vacation in Timbuktu while he's unhappy. Every season, even aging, has its rewards!

As another smart interviewee was quick to point out,

changes in goals in various seasons of life were made of her own will: "My goals changed as my life changed. I don't feel that I've sacrificed." That sentiment was true of all the smart women who talked about adaptations and detours in their plans. They were all quick to point out that life changes, and priorities and plans, change to meet those priorities. Smart women don't blame; they adapt.

From a successful woman who shows excitement about this new season of her life: "I'm just now going to work with agents. I'm also taking acting classes, I'm doing some plays, and I might do some commercials. I'm exploring. When I turned 50, I decided that I was going to wake up every morning and do something that made me happy and that would contribute something to the world. I think the first 50 years we have tremendous responsibilities and we're in the acquiring mode. But now I feel like it's time to give back. That's one of the reasons we work so hard — so we can get to the place that we can do what we *want* to do and not so much of what we *have* to do. That's where I am right now. I'm in this wonderful transition phase that says I can do more with my life than what I've done in the past."

Another smart woman sums up this way: "Enjoy the season you're in and recognize that the priorities you set for your life and what represents balance for you in a particular season will change. Enjoy that. Recognize that some of the frustrations and challenges you face as a younger woman go with the season. But these things are going to equip you to find greater joys in another season. Don't be afraid of growing older, because as you embrace each new season, it brings its own joys and new opportunities for fulfillment. Understanding that is making the rest of my life a lot easier."

Another successful woman in midlife remembers consciously dividing her life into segments of change: "I've always hoped for myself that I would be a person who changed. I don't want to stop growing. The thought of not changing frightens me. The things that give me the greatest pleasure are the experiences. It's not the material stuff. It's all the things that go through my mind, the internal data that

> *"Don't be afraid of growing older, because as you embrace each new season, it brings its own joys and new opportunities for fulfillment."*

comes in. I value the continuum of life, being in a different spot. I'm going through my own midlife crisis now, where I know I've got to make another change. It's not because of dissatisfaction about where I am. That's not what drives me. Life's like an amusement park. When kids get on the rides, then they don't want to get off. They just want to stay on the ride, and stay on the ride, and stay on the ride. I'm constantly saying, I want to get to the other rides. That's hard to do when you like the ride you're on. It's contradictory to the way we're raised — we're programmed to stability and non-change. But I want to move on, to change."

So What's To Fear About Aging?

Those who mentioned apprehension about growing older commented on gravity and falling faces and fannies. Most mentioned the prospect of being in bad health. But overwhelmingly, those surveyed say they have no real dread or fear of growing older.

One seventy-six-year-old responded, "There's just so much to do. I'm as busy after retirement as I was before. Growing old has its blessings."

One thirty-something says, "I can't wait to be forty. The women I know who are forty are mature and confident. They have secretly learned how to take care of themselves. They have so much to offer, so much energy, looks, poise."

Another thirty-something: "I'm really, really looking forward to aging. I hope I live to be 100. That's my goal. I think that the benefits that will come with that are going to be tremendous in terms of experience, wisdom, knowledge, and the opportunity we'll have to share with people who are behind us. They can say, 'Here's what worked for me; here's what didn't work for me.' I can remember when 60 was old. Now, at 60 you're just starting to live. Now, at 85 you're starting to get old."

Another thirty-something: "It was kind of funny growing up. I never saw myself as being past thirty. I had no vision of being married with kids, growing up, or being a professional and middle-aged. I couldn't even conceive of it. Now, I guess

I can picture that I will get old. I wouldn't mind the age if I could stay vigorous and healthy like these women you read about who are 100 and still dressed, living at home, being active. Like Jessica Tandy, who won her Oscar when she was 80. Nobody would mind being 80 if that's what it's like."

From another thirty-something: "I think life gets better. I'm waiting to turn 40, because I really think it's exciting. I'm 38 years old and have had a successful business. I've been a poor child from rural farms in Arkansas. I've had a life I couldn't even dream about, much less know it was there. So what I'm doing now is positioning myself to be even more comfortable later in life. To enjoy it. You can work hard for so long, and then you've got to relax and pull back and say, 'Let me try to figure out what I want to do next.' "

A forty-something ponders: "I have so much I want to do. I look at life as stages. In this stage of life I focus on this thing, and in that stage I'm going to focus on that thing."

From another forty-something: "Oh, I love the idea of aging — for what I know it's going to bring. Right now my stage is connected to parenting. When I'm finished with that, I'm sure I'll have enough energy to put into a whole, new something. Maybe the grandchildren bit, and the wisdom that comes with age."

A forty-seven-year-old: "I've thought this through many times. If you ask a three-year-old, she can't imagine life without Barbie. But you reach a time in your life when Barbie's not important. So part of getting older has to do with the thoughts and fears about being attractive and alluring to men. It's not so much the Barbie syndrome, but it's the joy or the mentality of what you're into. I think there are such wonderful things that come with getting older. I've enjoyed my youth. I've enjoyed my adulthood, and I'm going to have a great old time with the gray-haired campers."

A fifty-something becomes philosophical: "The wonderful thing about being in your fifties is that a lot of things have been settled one way or the other."

Another fifty-something: "I'm excited about it. The other day I wrote my autobiography from 1985 back. I wrote all the

> *"I look at life as stages. In this stage of life I focus on this thing, and in that stage I'm going to focus on that thing."*

things that I had done because I had my fiftieth birthday this year. Then I wrote what will happen with the next 35 years. I had the best time with it. I just made it up, based on what my dreams are, what I want to have happen and what I like. I'm excited about going into the new millennium. I'm so glad I'm alive right now."

Another fifty-something: "Maurice Chevalier said, 'Nobody wants to be 80 until he's 79.' I do think life's a laboratory. The things that you used to get stars for, you now just get a check mark. I love the verse in Psalms: 'Teach me to number my days so that I will gain a heart of wisdom.' It helps you make decisions much better, much faster. You know, we were invited to a party a while back, and I thought, 'Oh, that'll be fun. Okay, the party starts at 8:00. Half hour drive.' Then I thought, 'No, that's not something I want to spend five hours on.' That's the big thing about getting older — you do become much wiser in your decisions."

Finally, one smart woman recalls her step-grandmother as a role model for aging: "My father's mother had an operation to have her appendix out and died the first night home of a blood clot, leaving four small children. Then my grandfather remarried. While these two were on their honeymoon in California, he was killed in a car accident.

"His bride came back to raise the four stepchildren, whom she'd never really known or lived with yet. And when those four married and had children of their own, she would collect all the grandchildren for Sunday operas at her house. She cooked dinner and then played the operas on the record player as Sunday entertainment. As head of the home economics department at the University of Wyoming, she taught a class in growing old and invited foreign exchange students to live with her so they could go to the university. Then when she retired, she traveled around the world visiting these students."

What was her legacy? According to her granddaughter: "What she taught me when I was really young is that finances are only a very small part of life. She developed our love for music, for plays, for symphonies. You have to develop strength, and you have to develop interests, so that when you can retire, you blossom into those other areas. I guess my philosophy of growing old is modeled after hers — that you have a responsibility to grow the other interests in your life and to grow the spiritual side of your life. Then when you quit work, you don't drop dead because there's nothing left."

I don't know about you, but I don't hear disappointment, distress, or desperation in the voices of these maturing women. I hear excitement, promise, peace, plans, and contribution.

Time spent longing for the past and "the good old days" or longing for the future until "real" life begins is wasted time. Smart women swim in the seasons of life, enjoying each stage of the journey for its own thrills and commitments. They have a deep spiritual sense of who they are in the eternal scheme of things — and a belief system that does not limit and stifle, but throws open the window to all possibilities!

Appendix: Summary of Interviews

Education:
    No college degree: 9.6%
    College degree: 80.4%
    Advanced degrees: 43 %
    Doctorates: 11.7%

Titles:
    Professionals: 41 %
    Middle Managers: 27 %
    Senior Executives: 23.5%
    Entrepreneurs: 7.8%
    Not employed at present: 3.9%

Marital Status:
    Single, never married: 7.8%
    Single, divorced: 5.8%
    Married: 86.3%
    Multiple marriages: 23.5%

Children:
    Married/divorced   92 %
        with children:
    Married, no children: 7.8%

Race:
    Caucasian: 84.3%
    African American: 9.8%
    Asian: 3.9%
    Hispanic: 1.9%

Religion:
    Have a personal relationship
        with God: 72.5%
    Believe in Higher Power,
        seeking deeper understanding   15.6%
    No belief in Higher Power: 11.7%

OTHER RESOURCES BY DIANNA BOOHER

BOOKS

Get Ahead, Stay Ahead

Fresh-Cut Flowers for a Friend

Get a Life Without Sacrificing Your Career

*Communicate With Confidence: How To Say it Right the First Time
    and Every Time*

*Clean Up Your Act: Effective Ways To Organize Paperwork and
    Get It Out of Your Life*

Cutting Paperwork in the Corporate Culture

Executive's Portfolio of Model Speeches for All Occasions

First Thing Monday Morning

Would You Put That in Writing?

Good Grief, Good Grammar

The New Secretary: How To Handle People as Well as You Handle Paper

Send Me a Memo: A Handbook of Model Memos

The Complete Letterwriter's Almanac

To the Letter: A Handbook of Model Letters for the Busy Executive

Great Personal Letters for Busy People

Writing for Technical Professionals

Winning Sales Letters

67 Presentation Secrets to Wow Any Audience

VIDEOTAPES

Basic Steps for Better Business Writing (series)

Business Writing: Quick, Clear, Concise

Closing the Gap: Gender Communication Skills

Cutting Paperwork: Management Strategies

Cutting Paperwork: Support Staff Strategies

AUDIOTAPE SERIES

Get Your Book Published

People Power

Write to the Point: Business Communications From Memos to Meetings

SOFTWARE (DISKS AND CD-ROM)

Effective Writing

Effective Editing

Good Grief, Good Grammar

More Good Grief, Good Grammar

Ready, Set, NeGOtiate

Model Business Letters

Model Personal Letters

Model Sales Letters

Model Speeches & Toasts

WORKSHOPS

Effective Writing

Technical Writing

Developing Winning Proposals

Good Grief, Good Grammar

To-the-Point E-mail and Voice Mail

Customer Service Communications

Increasing Your Personal Productivity

Presentations That Work

People Power (interpersonal skills)

People Productivity (interpersonal skills)

Listening Until You Really Hear

Resolving Conflict Without Punching Someone Out

Leading and Participating in Productive Meetings

Negotiating So That Everyone Feels Like a Winner

SPEECHES

Communication: From Boardroom to Bedroom

Communication: The 10 Cs

The Gender Communication Gap: "Did You Hear What I Think I Said?"

Selling Across Gender Lines

Communicating CARE to Customers

Write This Way to Success

Platform Tips for the Presenter

Get a Life Without Sacrificing Your Career

You Are Your Future: Employable for a Lifetime

The Plan and the Purpose — Despite the Pain and the Pace

ABOUT THE AUTHOR

Dianna Booher is an internationally recognized business communication expert and the author of 32 books and numerous audios, videos, CD-ROM's, and an entire suite of software to increase communication effectiveness and productivity. She is the founder and president of Booher Consultants, based in the Dallas-Fort Worth metroplex. Her firm provides communication training to some of the largest Fortune 500 companies and government agencies: IBM, Exxon, Mobil, Hewlett-Packard, Honeywell, Texas Instruments, Pennzoil, AMR, Frito-Lay, Blue Cross and Blue Shield, Coopers & Lybrand, Dean Witter Reynolds, Deloitte & Touche, NASA, and MCI.

Dianna Booher and her staff travel internationally, speaking and presenting seminars and training workshops on communication and motivational topics.

If you woulkd like more infomration regarding scheduling a training workshop or if you would like to write to the author, address your correspondence to:

Booher Consultants, Inc.

4001 Gateway Dr.

Colleyville, TX 76034-5917

Phone: 817-318-6000

Booher@compuserve.com

Website: www.BooherConsultants.com

Additional copies of this book
are available from your
local bookstore.

Trade Life Books
Tulsa, Oklahoma